In this book Charles Larmore aims t
and pervasive forms of moral comple
neglected by moral and political philosophers. In the first place he
argues that virtue is not, as both Kantian and utilitarian theories
portray it, ⸺   Rather,
as Aris⸺   use of
judg⸺   ⸺en and how the rules as-
so⸺   ⸺e apply. However, Larmore does not endorse
the views of those neo-Aristotelian critics of liberalism (from the
German Idealists on) who have sought to restore the holism of the
polis. He argues – and this is the second pattern of complexity –
that recognizing the value of constitutive ties with shared forms of
life does not undermine the liberal ideal of political neutrality toward differing ideals of the good life. This is because moral considerations that may be decisive within the political realm need not
have the same priority in other areas of social life, and liberalism
is best considered a political doctrine, not a philosophy of man.
Finally Larmore argues for what he calls the heterogeneity of morality. Moral thinking need not in the end be exclusively deontological or consequentialist, or in any way monolithic, and we
should recognize that the ultimate sources of moral value are
diverse.

The arguments presented here do not attack the possibility of
moral theory. But in addressing some of the central issues of moral
and political thinking today they attempt to restore to that thinking
greater flexibility and a necessary sensitivity to our common
experience.

Patterns of moral complexity

Patterns of moral complexity

CHARLES E. LARMORE

COLUMBIA UNIVERSITY

CAMBRIDGE UNIVERSITY PRESS

CAMBRIDGE

NEW YORK   PORT CHESTER

MELBOURNE   SYDNEY

Published by the Press Syndicate of the University of Cambridge
The Pitt Building, Trumpington Street, Cambridge CB2 1RP
40 West 20th Street, New York, NY 10011-4211, USA
10 Stamford Road, Oakleigh, Victoria 3166, Australia

First published 1987
Reprinted 1988, 1992

Library of Congress Cataloging in Publication Data
Larmore, Charles E.
Patterns of moral complexity.
1. Ethics. I. Title.
BJ1012.L34 1987 170 86-17014

British Library Cataloguing in Publication Data
Larmore, Charles E.
Patterns of moral complexity.
1. Ethics
I. Title
170 BJ1012.L34

ISBN 0 521 33034 3 hardback
ISBN 0 521 33891 3 paperback

Transferred to digital printing 2001

To J. K. L. and to the memory of M. H. K.

NOUS avons perdu en imagination ce que nous avons gagné en connaissances; nous sommes par là même incapables d'une exaltation durable: les anciens étaient dans toute la jeunesse de la vie morale; nous traînons toujours après nous je ne sais quelle arrière-pensée qui naît de l'expérience, et qui défait l'enthousiasme.

–Benjamin Constant, *De l'esprit de conquête et de l'usurpation*

Contents

Contents

Preface

The goal of theory must be to discern some order in the welter of phenomena. This is as true of moral philosophy as it is of other forms of inquiry. However, moral theory in general and political theory in particular have been burdened, from their Greek beginnings through modern times, with unnecessarily simplistic notions of the overall order that they can expect to discover. As a result the genuine problems confronting moral philosophy have too often gone not merely unsolved, but also unperceived.

The aim of *Patterns of Moral Complexity* is to recover some of the complexity of the phenomena with which moral philosophers ought to deal. Of course, bare appeals to unmastered complexity are themselves rather simpleminded. Everyone knows that there is always something more to learn. So I must insist that the types of complexity with which I shall be concerned are fundamental and pervasive, not confined to any specific moral problem, but constitutive of morality in general. For this very reason I am reluctant to define at the outset just what I mean by "morality," since such definitions have usually turned out to be nothing less than theories that deny these very forms of complexity. What I have in mind will be best understood if I begin with at least a rough description of those neglected dimensions of morality that will be my theme.

The two dominant traditions of modern moral philosophy, Kantianism and utilitarianism, have been at one in seeking a fully explicit decision procedure for settling moral questions. As a result, they have missed the central role of moral judgment, or the faculty of insight into how general rules are to be applied to particular situations. Rules are, undeniably, a necessary feature of morality, but morality does not consist merely in the conscientious adherence to rules.

A second simplification that I shall attack involves the assumption that what may be a decisive moral consideration in one area of social life must carry an equal weight in other areas. Nowhere has this assumption played a more insistent and harmful role than in the domain of political theory. Since the Enlightenment it has shaped much of the debate about the foundations of liberalism. The fundamental liberal principle is that the state should remain neutral toward disputed and controversial ideals of the good life. If, however, a person believes that one ideal of the fulfilled life is preferable to another, how can he also believe, antiliberals have demanded, that the state should remain neutral between them?[1] To antiliberals, pleas for political neutrality have seemed to signify a lack of personal conviction, a loss of substance. At the same time liberals themselves, from Kant and Mill until today (including, at least in part, John Rawls), have often yielded to the same underlying simplification. They have supposed that the ideal of political neutrality ought to include a general commitment to "autonomy" or to "experimentalism" toward different forms of life, a demand that in general our deepest self-understanding ought thus to be independent of any concrete notion of the good life. Consequently, ever since the age of German Romanticism, the most widespread pattern of antiliberal thought has sought to turn this argumentative strategy to its own ends. Recognizing both the considerable disadvantages in the ideal of autonomy as well as the value of constitutive ties to shared, substantial forms of life, antiliberals have inferred that the political ideal of neutrality must also be unacceptable. In this way both sides to an ongoing debate about the foundations of liberalism have passed over an important dimension of moral complexity on which I intend to focus. Ideals that may continue to shape substantially our lives outside the political realm may be considerations from which we must abstract within that realm. For example, a full conception of human freedom may well include more that the "negative" freedom of governmental noninterference (it may refer to self-realization or the recognition of necessity). For a liberal, however, negative freedom may nonetheless remain all that should be politically relevant, since more substantial aspects of freedom belong at the heart of controversial ideals of the good life. What has thus been too often missed or misunderstood is the good reasons for the differentiation between the private and the public, *homme* and *citoyen*, or as I shall also say, between personal and political ideals. Antiliberals have generally rejected it because of their blinkered reliance upon simplistic sociology: They have assumed that a society must either be a whole, all of its parts animated by a common view of the good, or collapse into atomistic individualism.

The third and perhaps the most radical dimension of moral complexity that has usually been neglected lies in what I shall call the heterogeneity of morality. An abiding assumption of much of moral philosophy has been that ultimately there must be a single source of moral value. The continual controversy between "deontological" and "consequentialist" theories is an important example of this simplification. Kantians and utilitarians, the best-known protagonists of these two camps, have both supposed that in the last analysis the structure of morality must be *either* deontological (involving a set of absolute duties we must heed whatever others may do as a result of what we do) *or* consequentialist (demanding that we bring about the greatest good overall, so that what we ought to do depends on how we expect others to react to what we do). Another example is the frequent supposition that either *all* moral obligations must be "categorical" (in the sense of being binding on us whatever our empirically conditioned interests) or *none* are. Monism of this sort has usually presented itself less as a plausible working hypothesis than as something like a requirement of reason, a conviction that otherwise moral theory is a fruitless task. Theorizing, however, never benefits from demarcating in advance the boundaries of the intelligible. I shall argue that we do best to see morality, at its deepest level, as a motley of ultimate commitments. As a result we should acknowledge that moral conflict can be ineliminable.

These, then, are the dimensions of complexity that I want to put at the center of moral theory. Happily, it is not a task that must be carried out single-handedly. Although the general tendency has been to simplify away such complexity, the history of moral philosophy also harbors significant and fertile exceptions. (The history of moral theory is no less complex an affair than morality itself.) Indicating what these exceptions are will also provide a useful occasion for outlining the overall structure of this book.

Greek ethical thought is an invaluable resource for correcting the one-sided emphasis upon rules that characterizes so much of modern moral philosophy. One of the best introductions to the function of judgment and to its significance for other moral phenomena such as character and virtue lies in Aristotle's discussion of φρόνησις, or moral judgment. This is one area, therefore, where the passage from ancient to modern moral thought has brought a diminished appreciation for the complexity of practical reason. The function of moral judgment and the reasons for the modern neglect of it are the subjects of Chapter 1.

But there remain many areas of morality where Aristotle's writings do not offer a suitable model for moral theory. (For example, I shall argue that judgment ought to play a greater role in personal than in political morality.) Consequently, I have mixed feelings toward the contemporary rebirth of Aristotelianism in ethics. Neither Aristotle nor Greek ethical theory in general displayed any real grasp of the other two dimensions of moral complexity. Believing that reasonable people will agree upon a single vision of the good life and that thus the task of the state must be to express this common understanding, Aristotle had no room for a differentiation between political ideals and personal ideals. Indeed, his model of the polis has served as one of the great sources of inspiration for antiliberal thought since the end of the eighteenth century. Aristotle was similarly blind to the radical heterogeneity of morality. To him moral conflict seems always to have been a mark of our ignorance, not a reflection of the moral order. One of the aims of this book, therefore, is to set the limits to what we should assimilate from Aristotle. I shall try to explain to what extent liberals should be Aristotelians. In Chapter 2 I discuss the central deficiencies of Aristotelian ethics by examining the most notable neo-Aristotelian tract in recent years, Alasdair MacIntyre's *After Virtue*.

These other two dimensions of moral complexity are ones that, as I have said, modern moral theory as well has too often neglected. So it is fortunate that to this generalization, too, there exist important exceptions. Although liberal political theory since Kant and Mill has usually presented itself as an all-encompassing moral theory committed to overall personal ideals such as autonomy or an experimental attitude toward ways of life, earlier liberals had a better understanding of the liberal separation of social spheres.

More than a century of religious civil war led seventeenth century thinkers such as Locke (as it had already led sixteenth century thinkers like Bodin) to insist upon two distinct but interrelated ideas that never played more than a minor role in ancient and medieval thought. One was the *pluralist* conviction that there exist many different but independently and even equally valuable conceptions of the good life; the other was the need for *toleration* because reasonable people are likely to disagree about what belongs to the good life. (The distinction between these two ideas consists in the fact that pluralism has to do not with disagreement about ideals, but with agreement about the independent and equal value of different ideals.) Bodin and Locke believed that reasonable people are bound to differ and disagree about the religious meaning of life. They were among the first, we might say, to challenge the axiom that reason tends naturally toward single solutions and unanimity of opinion, that difference and disagreement signal a failure of reason.[2] So they concluded that the state must be based on principles that abstract from religious ideals, which nonetheless retain their significance in other areas of life.

This insight into the separate concerns of different social spheres makes early modern theories of religious toleration a better model for liberal theory than most of what the late eighteenth and nineteenth centuries have to offer. What is ultimately of value in Locke's political theory is not his ideas about natural rights and property (which have been the focus of most recent commentary), but rather this general method of abstraction and specialization. This method provides the basis on which we should understand the extension of pluralism and toleration beyond the religious sphere that is the concern of modern liberalism. In this way we can circumvent one of the damaging paradoxes of later liberal theory, namely, its defense of political neutrality by appeal to ideals of the person that are themselves rightly controversial. Because liberalism is fundamentally a response to the variety and controversiality of ideals of the good life, it needs a justification of political neutrality that is itself appropriately neutral. In Chapter 3 I try to work out such a justification. Then in Chapters 4 and 5 I develop more the idea of the differentiation of personal and political ideals. I shall attempt to show that we have no good reason to accept the Kantian version of liberalism, but also that the dominant pattern of antiliberalism since the French Revolution, which I call political romanticism, has been of mixed theoretical value: Political romantics have provided some genuine insights into defects of the Kantian ideal of autonomy, but they have produced no good arguments against the ideal of political neutrality.

What I have termed the heterogeneity of morality is also a phenomenon to which not every theorist has been blind. Moral conflict and the "fragmentation" of moral value lie at the center of recent writings by Stuart Hampshire, Thomas Nagel, and Bernard Williams, to which I am much indebted, although not without disagreements.[3] There is also the outstanding example of Max Weber, who insisted upon the irreducible plurality of "value-spheres." Distinguishing between "an ethics of conviction" and an "ethics of responsibility" (a distinction that corresponds, in effect, to that between deontological and consequentialist perspectives), he argued that neither ethic should be rejected, that we must learn to live with both, and with the conflicts between them. This is the insight that lay behind his much-misunderstood concept of *Zweck-rationalität*. It differs from what he called *Wertrationalität*, not (as Weber's critics have complained) by being narrowly "instrumental" and dependent upon arbitrarily given ends, but rather by being aware of the existence of rival yet ultimate moral ends, and thus of the possible moral costs of pursuing any one of them.[4] The heterogeneity of morality, along with the writings of some of those who have acknowledged it, forms the subject of Chapter 6.

Contrasts of the sort I have drawn between theory and phenomena may suggest to some readers that I am committed to some substantial version of what philosophers call moral realism, that is, to the view that actions and persons have moral properties in some way independent of what anyone at all thinks about them. But this impression would be wrong. I prefer to suspend judgment about questions of moral ontology, although I shall have occasion to defend the objectivity of moral reasoning.[5] (That ontology and objectivity can be separate matters would seem to be confirmed by the case of mathematics.) By the phenomena I mean our well-considered moral commitments. And so in urging that moral theory become adequate to the complexity of the phenomena, I shall be arguing that moral theory must begin on the basis of the moral knowledge we already have.

C. L.

Acknowledgments

In writing this book I have been helped by a great many people and institutions. It was in a discussion group with Norbert Hornstein and Robert Amdur in the early 1980s that I began to get a clearer idea of the complexities of political liberalism. I am indebted to all those who read part or all of the manuscript – Bruce Ackerman, Louis Begley, Raymond Geuss, Stephen Holmes, Norbert Hornstein, Isaac Levi, David Luban, Odo Marquard, Glenn Most, Thomas Pogge, Enno Rudolph, Michael Sandel, James Walsh, and Bernard Williams. My greatest intellectual debts are to Stephen Holmes and Glenn Most, for more than a decade of comradeship, and to Niklas Luhmann, whose influence on this book, too often unacknowledged, will be plain to those who know his work.

Portions of this book have been given as talks at the Universität Bielefeld (West Germany), the Institut für die Wissenschaft vom Menschen (Vienna), and the New School for Social Research. I am grateful to these audiences for their interest and criticisms. I am also thankful for the support that the Columbia University Council for Research in the Humanities has offered me over a number of summers. Earlier versions of parts of this book appeared in the following places: Chapter 1 in *The Review of Metaphysics* (vol. 35, no. 2, December 1981), the last section of Chapter 5 in *The Journal of Philosophy* (vol. 81, no. 6, June 1984), and Chapter 6 in *Einheit als Grundfrage der Philosophie* (Darmstadt: Wissenschaftlich Buchgesellschaft, 1985), edited by K. Gloy and E. Rudolph. I thank the editors of these publicatons for their permission to reprint this material.

It is a great pleasure to thank Jonathan Sinclair-Wilson of Cambridge University Press and Marilyn Prudente of Comprehensive Graphics for their kindness and support during the preparation of this book. I am incalculably indebted to my typist Mary Nunez not only for her expertise, but also for her detection of some very bad sentences.

Finally, the debt I owe my wife Amey goes far beyond this book, but without her I would never have finished it.

Chapter 1

Moral judgment – an Aristotelian insight

KANT ON EXAMPLES

In this chapter I want to reestablish an Aristotelian insight that modern moral theories have systematically neglected. It is the importance of judgment, or what Aristotle called φρόνησις, in moral deliberation. However, I shall begin by discussing the question of what role examples may have in moral experience. This strategy is only apparently circuitous. The role assigned to examples is symptomatic of how much the significance of moral judgment is appreciated, because the use of examples forms one way in which judgment is exercised. Indirectly, then, I shall be trying to rehabilitate the significance of examples in moral deliberation. But my chief aim will be to establish the centrality of judgment in moral deliberation and to explain why there has been so much resistance to recognizing it.

A familiar view of moral examples gives them, we might say, a rhetorical rather than a logical role. This view prevails in modern ethical theories. Examples, it is urged, have the task of persuading us to do our duty. They excite the imagination and the passions in a way in which, supposedly, moral rules and reason in general are less able to do; and since most of us are not motivated most of the time by rules and reason alone, examples serve an indispensable function. Observe that this view treats examples only as a means for motivating us to act in accord with what has already been determined to be our duties in the situation at hand. What

1

our duties are and which actions will satisfy them is supposed to be a matter that the moral rules themselves suffice to decide. In other words, this view does not allow examples to play any role in the determination of what is morally right; examples serve only to motivate *people*, for whom *knowledge* of what is morally right does not form the sole claim upon their attention. This was the understanding of moral examples that, in the *Groundwork of the Metaphysics of Morals*, Kant was quite right to consider as one that makes them extrinsic to the structure of moral duty itself. "Every example of morality presented to me," Kant wrote, thinking of examples as this traditional view conceives of them," must first itself be judged by moral principles in order to decide if it is fit to serve as an original example."[1] Hence, not only do examples thus conceived have nothing to do with ascertaining what our duties are, but our choice of examples amounts to no more than applying the rules contained in the concept of those duties. For a purely rational being, one motivated by moral considerations alone, moral examples would be unnecessary.

Kant's conception of examples is more complex, however, than what I have described so far. Only after going through his full position will we be able to perceive the way in which he failed to understand the importance of judgment in moral deliberation.

It will be recalled that in the *Critique of Pure Reason*, just before the chapter on schematism, Kant wrote of a faculty that he called "native wit" (*Mutterwitz*) or judgment. Concepts, he had argued, are best thought of as rules; thus, the concept "table" should be construed as the rule we employ for classifying certain things as tables. But, he argued, an understanding of how to apply that rule cannot consist merely in the mastery of further rules, since that would only transform the problem into one of how those further rules can be applied. The ability to apply rules must rest ultimately, he insisted, on a different kind of ability, itself not a rule-governed procedure, but one by which we simply see that a thing falls within the scope of a rule. This sort of knack

2

Kant called judgment. Furthermore, he claimed that this faculty of judgment, while impervious to being instructed by any set of rules, could be improved through the use of examples – examples of the rules being applied in concrete cases. "Examples are thus the go-cart of judgment; and those who are lacking in the general talent [of applying rules] can never dispense with them."[2]

In the light of this observation about judgment and examples in the First Critique, we may be surprised by the rather severe disapproval that Kant showed toward the use of examples in moral deliberation. There are two reasons for Kant's attitude toward examples in his moral philosophy: The one has to do with the peculiarities of his idea of moral freedom, whereas the other concerns what is the fundamental deficiency in Kant's theory of judgment. In the *Critique of Practical Reason*, there is a section entitled "Von der Typik der reinen praktischen Urteilskraft" that deals with the problem of how we apply general moral rules to particular cases.[3] According to Kant, such application must proceed in the following way. We must first determine whether an action could fall under a law of nature; that is, we must first discover whether it agrees with a universalizable maxim in accordance with which it may have been willed, not freely but for empirically conditioned reasons. And then, in order to understand it as a moral action, we must conceive of it as having been willed freely. Kant believed, of course, that there is nothing in experience that can ever tell us whether an action was willed freely. Freedom is only a possibility that we add in thought to what experience discloses. That means, Kant argued, that the only general concept that in effect is being applied is the one whereby we view the action as conforming to a law of nature (a law of psychology). Thus, the only kinds of examples required by judgment in this case will be not *moral* examples, but examples of kinds of actions that may or may not be moral. There can be no examples of free action.

There are a number of difficulties in Kant's argument. An immediate objection is that Kant seems to have overlooked here the important distinction between morally *right* action, in which the performance of duty consists, and morally *good* action, which reflects the motive with which one's duty is done. An action may be right, even if not good, so long as it conforms to what was the person's duty in the circumstances. He may, after all, do the right thing for the wrong reason. Thus, whether or not Kant was correct to claim that there can be no examples of morally good action (action motivated by moral freedom), he ought to have agreed on the basis of his general point about concept-application in the First Critique that examples of morally right action may indeed play an indispensable role in moral experience. That is, they may aid judgment in determining whether the action fits the moral rule expressed by a universalizable maxim. Even the purely moral agent would require judgment, and thus might need examples, to apply moral rules to particular circumstances; he, too, could not replace such use of examples by the use of rules picking them out, since examples of this sort would make possible his very application of those rules.

We must do more, however, than merely revise Kant's strictures against moral examples to fit the general theory of judgment and examples that he presented in the First Critique. My main thesis is that, at least for the moral realm, the general theory itself is fundamentally incomplete. It rests on the assumption that the rules definitive of some concept suffice by themselves to determine whether something falls under that concept; judgment is merely our capacity actually to apply such rules, to see something as the sort of thing those rules pick out.

However, it is not always true that moral rules have enough content to settle by themselves whether something falls under their concept. It is not always true that judgment has no other task than simply to *see* that moral rules indeed suffice to identify the things of which the concept may be predicated. Modern moral theory in its two principal forms, Kantianism and utilitarianism, has urged that what is morally right can be fully specified by rules. Indeed, this demand for a fully explicit decision-procedure was a reaction to what

4

modern moralists perceived as the intolerable vagueness of Aristotle's appeals to φρόνησις.[4] Their hope is redeemable, however, only at the cost that morality cease to be very much like what it has been and still is. There are moral duties whose rules by themselves cannot sufficiently determine whether in particular circumstances these duties have a claim on what we should do and, if so, what actions would satisfy these duties. Because this is so, judgment (and examples) must play a far more substantial role in the application of moral rules to concrete cases than envisaged either in Kant's moral theory (as I have so far reassembled it)[5] or in utilitarian ethics. I shall now turn to a more systematic account of the substantial role that judgment must play in moral deliberation. Much of my discussion will be guided by Aristotle's treatment of φρόνησις.

THE CENTRALITY OF JUDGMENT

There are some moral duties, such as keeping promises or paying back debts, whose rules allow little leeway for individual moral judgment in particular circumstances. Marginal are the cases where there may be some dispute about whether one is obligated to keep a promise one has made or about how that promise is to be rightly kept. Naturally if I have promised to return to someone today a book that I have borrowed, that promise leaves open whether to return it in the morning or the afternoon. But in this case the schematic area of the moral rule is not morally relevant: Insofar as no other moral duties are involved, the choice among the alternatives left open is morally indifferent. The decision when today to return the book does not, therefore, call for moral judgment, but rather for nonmoral considerations (convenience, for example). By contrast, moral duties like courage, generosity, and benevolence are duties whose rules appear too schematic to settle by themselves when those duties are incumbent upon us and how they are (in a moral sense) correctly to be carried out. For duties of this sort moral judgment is indispensable.

It will be helpful to begin by distinguishing two dimensions along which this second kind of duty calls for moral judgment. First of all, we must determine whether our particular circumstances are ones in which such a duty has a claim on what we are to do. Secondly, even if we believe that our situation thus forces a certain duty upon us, we must figure out which available course of action best satisfies this duty. For the kinds of duties I have in mind, both decisions require moral judgment, a sense of the moral requirements and possibilities of the situation that goes beyond what the rules by themselves can tell us. Let us consider courage, for example. We might define the duty of courage as the duty to defend or pursue what is important to us in the face of obstacles that make this difficult or dangerous, although neither futile nor suicidal. But such a general rule cannot tell us by itself whether a particular situation is one that requires us to defend and pursue our commitments, or one whose challenge to our commitments is relatively insignificant. Courage is a duty when the situation itself is important enough to call for it. This too is a clause belonging to the rule defining courage. But it is a clause that can be satisfied only by the exercise of moral judgment.

Now, even once we have come to believe that the situation is significant enough to be met with courage, we must still decide what specifically we should do to fulfill this duty. Here we can, of course, fall back on our practical knowledge concerning the likelihood that various actions will succeed in protecting or advancing our commitments. But we must, above all, determine what degree of intensity or tenacity in the defense of our commitments would be appropriate in a courageous response to the given situation. There are no general rules that will prove very helpful in our need to weigh the importance to us of our commitments against what we perceive the situation to require. Here moral judgment must steer us between the twin dangers of timidity and overzealousness, of doing too little to uphold our commitments and

6

of rushing headlong into extravagance. This situation calls for *moral* judgment because, unlike the case of determining when today I should return the book I promised to return today, the alternatives among which I have to decide admit of being morally better or worse.

Of course, judgment itself is not restricted to the moral domain, but is a general faculty concerned with the appropriate application of general rules (which may be more or less schematic) to particular situations. Moral judgment, with which I am alone concerned, aims at the appropriate application of *moral* rules to particular circumstances insofar as their application requires choosing among *morally* different alternatives. The particular task that duties like courage present to moral judgment arises from the schematic character of the rules associated with these duties. I would suggest that this is not primarily because these rules provide only necessary, but not sufficient, conditions for the application of the relevant moral concept. Their schematic character seems to lie rather in their stipulating that the situation must be "significant" or "important" enough and that our action must be a "fitting" way of carrying out our duty. Thus, generosity is a duty when the need of the person concerned is significant and especially when the person stands in a significant relation to us (e.g., as friend or previous benefactor), and we must carry out this duty by giving what is fitting, neither too little nor too much. It is the apparently ineliminable appeal in moral duties of this sort to what is significant and to what is fitting that connects them with the exercise of moral judgment.

An important objection to what I have asserted about the relation between moral judgment and general moral rules is that we give reasons for what we judge to be appropriate and that we can believe these are reasons only if there are *further* general rules that show that they are so. Suppose I conclude, for example, that generosity dictates that I help someone who is not likely to get assistance from elsewhere and who I believe deserves my help in virtue of some special relation in which we stand to each other. Surely, it will be argued, my judgment that this person deserves my help, if it is not to be arbitrary, will be based on reasons, and any such reason will in effect embody a rule by which judgment is operating. But here some important distinctions must be drawn. Either in having those reasons I am indeed applying a rule, but then the rule (e.g., as a friend, X deserves more consideration than an ordinary acquaintance) will generally be schematic enough to require judgment for its interpretation in the particular circumstances; or the rule embodied in the reasons I have for judging as I do is a rule that was not given in advance (and so is not in any sense being applied), but *emerges only in virtue of* the fact that having appraised the situation as I did I find those reasons compelling. This may be the case when the rule involved is a general one, but it will frequently be the case when the implied rule is quite specific (e.g., given everything that we have been through, X deserves this of me). This distinction between applying rules and acting on reasons that imply rules not given in advance is vital if we are to grasp the sense in which moral judgment responds to the particularity of a situation by going beyond the given content of the general rules that it applies. Observe that this distinction does not correspond to the one between explicit and implicit application of rules, since the latter implies that the rules were given in advance, but because of habituation did not figure in the agent's awareness. It may nonetheless be asked how anyone can perceive reasons *as* reasons, except in virtue of some rule that makes them so. But this question wrongly supposes that to have reasons for a belief I must have reasons for those reasons. Reasons must come to an end somewhere, although this does not imply that where reasons end we have reached the bedrock of self-evidence and indubitability (far from it in the case of moral judgment!). The importance of moral examples, I suggest, lies in their suitability as just such reasons, since they exemplify the exercise of moral judgment. A further question is how judgment operates in perceiving reasons for its decisions, a difficult question to which I shall turn in the last two sections of this chapter. For now, I hope it is clear what I mean by saying that in applying general moral rules to particular circumstances moral judgment consists in our ability to go beyond what those schematic rules alone can tell us about our duties.[6]

Although the two dimensions of moral deliberation that draw on our individual judgment – deciding what duties we must honor and what actions will best satisfy them – must be distinguished, it does not follow that in our deliberations we should always consider the two questions independently. It would often be rash to conclude that in a particular situation I do have a duty that must be honored, until I have ascertained what are the actual ways I have of carrying out that duty. This is because the available alternatives for satisfying that duty may themselves frustrate the satisfaction of other duties that I believe to have a stronger claim on me. In other words, we must be prepared to encounter moral conflicts.[7] Moreover, this phenomenon of moral conflict forms in itself another area in which moral judgment often plays an essential role. Of course, we do possess higher-order moral principles such as utility, or Kantian universalizability, one of whose tasks is to adjudicate moral conflicts. But many times the verdicts rendered by these higher-order principles for a particular case diverge, and then – because there are no higher rules to be invoked and because no *absolute* ranking of these principles is plausible – judgment may have to direct us how to choose. Thus, one action may recommend itself in virtue of its likelihood to produce a greater general happiness than the other alternatives, but because it involves knowingly injuring an innocent person, we may not be able to reconcile its performance with Kant's universalizability test. If a reasoned decision is possible in such a situation, moral judgment will be required.

The role that judgment plays in moral conflict differs importantly from the form that it assumes in the areas we have examined so far. In the previous cases, moral rules were too schematic to determine whether in any concrete case an obligation had to be honored and, if so, in what way. The kind of moral conflict with which we are now concerned sets moral

9

judgment, which as such we may view as our ability to make moral choices in the application of general moral rules to particular situations, precisely the opposite task. Higher-order moral principles, like utility, or Kantian universalizability represent attempts to specify the general concept of "the moral perspective" in terms of rules for moral decision making. The relation between these higher-order rules and the general concept with which they are associated is not (as before) that they are too schematic, but rather that each of them is too narrow. That is why in particular situations each of these higher-order rules may neglect and even exclude moral considerations that are urged by the others. That is also why, if a reasoned choice is possible, it is judgment that must determine what morality requires of us in such situations.

Despite his understanding of φρόνησις Aristotle showed little awareness of moral conflict, so he missed this specific role of moral judgment. Modern moral philosophy, with its desire for explicit and univocal decision-procedures, has stubbornly assumed that moral conflicts must be only apparent, that there must be some single higher-order principle that captures our most basic intuitions. Indeed, when moral theories of this monistic sort have run up against recalcitrant moral intuitions that conflict with their favored higher-order principle, they have too often resorted to the tactic of denying those intuitions their very status as "moral" ones. (Recall the charges of squeamishness and rule-worship that many utilitarians have leveled against those who morally reject an action knowingly injuring another, even though it happens to maximize the general happiness; recall also the censure of principlelessness that Kantians have often directed toward those who have held that sometimes a great good should be obtained at the price of doing evil.) Only when we suspend the monistic assumption underlying so much of moral theory, only when we acknowledge that not everything is good or right to the extent that it is commensurable with respect to any single standard, will we be able to recognize that even our understanding of what *the moral viewpoint* enjoins upon us in particular situations can call for the exercise of judgment. In many cases only moral judgment can guide us through "the fragmentation of value"[8] or what I shall call the heterogeneity of morality. In many cases, also, judgment will be powerless to settle the conflict.

About radical moral conflict I shall have much more to say in the last chapter of this book. Here I would like to sketch one further point directly connected with the phenomenon of judgment. Earlier I distinguished two kinds of moral duty – the kind whose rules are substantial enough to determine by themselves when (prima facie) that duty has a claim on our action, and the kind whose rules, being schematic, call for the exercise of judgment. My suggestion is that the ability to recognize and satisfy duties of the second kind (generosity, courage) is more readily associated with the idea of *virtue*. I do not mean to deny that someone showing a lack of concern toward his promises or debts could only exceptionally be said to have a virtuous character. But the performance of this sort of duty offers by itself little evidence of virtue. Before explaining this connection between virtue and duties that require judgment, I must say something about how I understand the notion of virtue. An ethics of virtue is often, but not very perspicuously, contrasted with an ethics of duty. The contrast elaborated by H. A. Prichard earlier in this century remains the clearest of such attempts. He argued that a virtuous action is done not from a sense of obligation (as an ethics of duty would require), but rather "willingly or with pleasure, ... from some desire which is intrinsically good, as arising from some intrinsically good emotion" (e.g., sympathy).[9] There is indeed a fairly clear distinction between the two motives of a sense of obligation and a feeling of sympathy. But Prichard is wrong to say that virtuous action stems only from the latter, at least if Aristotle's treatment of virtue is to be taken (as it is by Prichard) as paradigmatic. Aristotle understood both motives as necessary ingredients in virtuous action: His claim that temperance is more fully a virtue than continence or control over one's bad desires implies that virtuous action springs from more than just a sense of obligation, but his assertion that a person acts virtuously only if he knows what he is doing and chooses it for its own sake refers unmistakably to all that a sense of obligation need mean, namely a desire to do what is right because it is right.[10] I shall follow Aristotle in regarding virtuous action as dependent upon both sorts of motives together. It is action done because it is right and willingly so.

Now the special connection between virtue and duties requiring judgment can be explained thus. Virtue is a matter of character, a firm disposition to act virtuously. Paying back one's debts or keeping one's promises does not generally engage one's character in any very challenging way. It is perfectly obvious what one ought to do, even to someone who gives little thought to the demands of the moral life. To obtain a good idea of someone's moral virtue, we generally look to his capacity for moral imagination, in order to ascertain just how great an intrinsic interest he takes in doing what is right. That is because moral imagination is the ability to elaborate and appraise different courses of action that are only schematically determined by the given content of moral rules, in order to learn what in a particular situation is indeed the morally best thing to do. It expresses therefore a far more active and thoughtful interest in the moral life than does the observance of fully determinate moral rules. Moral imagination, however, clearly involves the exercise of moral judgment. Consequently, the fact that certain duties require moral imagination and moral judgment in order to be recognized and satisfied explains why these are the duties that we commonly associate with virtue. (The fact that an action required moral judgment, of course does not entail that the agent was acting virtuously since he might have exercised his judgment for an ulterior nonmoral, or even immoral, end; but the exercise of judgment offers one of the best sorts of evidence for virtue.)

By overlooking the importance of judgment, modern moral theories have presented a desiccated view of virtue.[11] Kant and Mill understood virtue simply as conscientious adherence to rules and principles, and so they seem never to have discerned that some duties show more about one's virtue than others. Indeed, their picture of the virtuous man seems modeled on the faithful promise-keeper. It fails to capture the way in which the exercise of virtue, through imagination and judgment, is an organ of moral discovery.

In *The Metaphysics of Morals* Kant half-perceived this point, in striking contrast to his earlier works in moral philosophy, which I discussed before. In this later treatise he distinguished between two kinds of moral duties that correspond to those that I have sought to distinguish: duties (like promise keeping or truth telling) that command simply that we perform certain actions, and duties (like generosity or gratitude) that enjoin us, he claimed, to act with the maxim of performing these duties for their own sake. Understandably Kant connected duties of the second kind with the idea of virtue, calling them *Tugendpflichten*, although he gave no general explanation why the performance of these duties, in contrast to the others, should require the agent to be acting from moral motives, and thus virtuously. The reason I have suggested for this fact is that these are duties whose ascertainment and whose satisfaction require the exercise of moral judgment and that this provides evidence for an intrinsic interest in doing what is right. Oddly enough, in this later work Kant had the materials at hand for just such an explanation. Duties of virtue he called "imperfect duties," in contrast to the "perfect duties" of the first sort, because they allow a certain leeway for their observance. The rule associated with such a duty, he wrote, cannot completely specify what actions should be done to satisfy that duty.[12] And at one point, although at one point only, Kant recognized that for the performance of such duties judgment is therefore required, a statement that thus seems to go beyond the too narrow theory of judgment presented in the First Critique.[13] But he promptly added that here the exercise of judgment will consist in the application of a further maxim, and so he concluded that ethics is concerned, not so much with judgment as with reason, or the application of principles.[14] With this Kant retreated to his earlier and narrower conception of judgment, ignoring what he himself had rightly come to understand about imperfect duties. So we cannot say that Kant had any more than a glimpse of the importance of moral judgment and its connection with virtue.[15]

THE PUZZLING NATURE OF JUDGMENT

I have been trying so far to plot the areas of moral experience in which judgment appears indispensable. Judgment is very far from being a marginal phenomenon. We might say fairly that *moral disagreement* arises chiefly in areas where judgment must be exercised. Usually our disagreements fix not upon the validity of general moral rules, but rather upon whether the rules are being properly applied, how they are to be satisfied, and what to do when they come into conflict; if the disagreement is about some moral rule, it centers around whether more general rules, when properly applied, entail the validity of this rule. Judgment offers us the way to resolve these disagreements by argument, by appeals to reasons. Because we should not suppose that the exercise of such judgment must itself consist in the application of (further) rules, we must recognize that "technical reason," or the application of fully determinate rules, and arbitrariness do not exhaust the ways in which we make decisions, at least in our moral experience. Indeed, it is the widespread assumption that all decisions that are not arbitrary must arise from the exercise of technical reason that has blinded so many modern philosophers to the importance, and even the existence, of moral judgment and thus to some of the real difficulties that we experience in moral decision making. (Of course, some decisions cannot escape being arbitrary because there are no reasons to prefer any of the alternatives.)[16]

Nonetheless, I have still said very little about just how judgment itself works. Although judgment can appeal to reasons, it does not do so by virtue of any general rules that make them reasons. The nature of moral judgment is a peculiarly difficult phenomenon to describe, partly because the tradition of moral philosophy, by so often neglecting the importance of judgment, has handed down to us so few attempts to make sense of it. But the difficulty has deeper roots than the paucity of philosophical resources at our disposal. After examining some earlier attempts to understand the nature of moral judgment, I shall turn to the question whether, by its nature, moral judgment is resistant to theoretical analysis.

The very idea of moral judgment we associate with Aristotle's discussion of φρόνησις. It has inspired much of what I have said so far. Reacting against what he perceived to be Plato's belief that virtue consists solely in the knowledge of general principles, Aristotle protested that moral action depends on the exercise of judgment in applying these principles to particular circumstances. Judgment itself, he stressed, is not an activity governed by general rules; instead, it must always respond to the peculiarities of the given situation (τὰ πρὸς τὸν καιρὸν σκοπεῖν).[17] Thus, no one can acquire judgment by being imparted some kind of formal doctrine. It can be learned only through practice, through being trained in the performance of right actions. That is why Aristotle wrote that we become just by doing just actions. Because training and experience play such a vital role in the acquisition of judgment, the development of moral character depends upon the moral life of the community.[18] Virtue depends on belonging – this is an Aristotelian insight that I shall examine at greater length in Chapter 5. This is what Aristotle had to say about the context in which moral judgment is acquired and the task that it performs. Significant about his account of judgment is that it contains very little about the precise way in which judgment is exercised. There is the famous doctrine of the mean. But recall that virtue, as the mean between opposing vices, is not a mean that can be calculated through the use of a general rule, but rather a mean "relative to us," namely a mean that according to Aristotle is what the person of judgment must determine with an eye to the particularity of the situation.[19] By calling virtue a mean Aristotle meant only that virtuous action is neither too little nor too much (in what we are to do and feel), but rather just what the situation required. He did suggest some rules of thumb for determining the mean "relative to us," but only judgment can shape their vagueness into meaningful directives:

1. We should endeavor to avoid that extreme that we are more inclined by nature to pursue;

2. We should learn what errors we typically make, in order better to avoid them in the future; and

3. We should be on our guard against the lures of pleasure.[20]

Aristotle's theory of the "practical syllogism" also sheds little light upon the nature of the exercise of moral judgment. The major and minor premises of the moral syllogism (whose conclusion is the action to be done) express, respectively, the duty to be performed and the way it can be fulfilled in the given circumstances – the good and the possible, as the *De Motu Animalium* (701a24) puts it.[21] These premises correspond to the two dimensions of moral judgment that I distinguished at the beginning of the previous section. But this means that the exercise of moral judgment precedes the inference from these premises; it consists in arriving at them in the first place. Thus, we cannot take the practical syllogism itself as a model of how moral judgment works. Perhaps Aristotle's most illuminating remark about the nature of moral judgment lay after all in the statement that "the decision lies with perception" (εν τη αισθήσει η κρίσις),[22] where by "αἴσθησις" he meant an understanding of the particularity of a situation. About *what* moral judgment is he really had no more to say.

Aristotle's notion of judgment was largely forgotten by modern moralists (from the sixteenth to the middle twentieth century), who preferred to see the moral life as simply the conscientious adherence to rules. The grounds for this neglect are complex and various. One was political: The technical construal of morality ensured that the moral life would be equally accessible to all, and not tied to some inscrutable know-how of the aristocracy. This was a worthy political end (for judgment is not the peculiar property of any class), but the cost of inappropriate means was high. Another ground was the more philosophical one that we are now pursuing – the difficulty in understanding how in fact judgment is exercised, a difficulty largely due to the special prestige that the technical idea of reason has enjoyed in modern times. An appreciation of judgment remained among some early modern political writers, in Guicciardini for example, but seldom elsewhere.[23]

One of the few moral philosophers in modern times to have acknowledged the importance of judgment in moral experience was Adam Smith in *The Theory of Moral Sentiments*. In the last section of the book he castigated the modern moralists for having forgotten what the ancient moralists had known – that "the rules of justice are the only rules of morality which are precise and accurate... [while] those of all the other virtues are loose, vague, and indeterminate."[24] (I shall return to this contrast between the political virtue of justice and the other virtues at the beginning of Chapter 3.) In contrast with what he saw as modern efforts to reduce casuistically the virtues to precise rules, Smith counseled that we should follow the practice of the ancients and conceive of the virtues in two related although inherently schematic ways. There is, first of all, the general rule or way of acting that we associate with a certain virtue. But because such a general rule must prove vague and imprecise, we must supplement it, Smith urged, with an idea of the characteristic sentiment upon which that virtue is founded. Smith's idea was that we might grasp the nature of moral judgment itself by examining the characteristic sentiment that, in addition to an understanding of some general rule, motivates the exercise of a particular virtue.[25] Nonetheless, he himself promptly conceded that the sentiment characteristic of a virtue (for example, the special concern one should feel for the welfare of a friend) undergoes a wide range of variation from circumstance to circumstance, and in any case a general description of that sentiment tends to portray it as the felt recognition of the associated general rule. On Smith's account as well, we find ourselves little nearer to an analysis of what moral judgment itself is. His view never really advanced beyond the assertion that proper moral judgment should be seen as the expression of the moral sentiment that "the impartial spectator" would feel.[26]

In recent years the Aristotelian idea of judgment has sometimes met with a more hospitable reception than before. Hans-Georg Gadamer, for example, has explicitly appealed to Aristotle's account of φρόνησις as a paradigm both of moral reasoning and of the interpretation of texts.[27] What, however, does Gadamer have to say about the nature of moral judgment, about the way in which it is exercised? Following Aristotle, he insists that we must not construe it as the implementation of a method. That would be to confuse moral (and aesthetic) judgment with the "technical," thoroughly rule-governed organization of experience that for him is characteristic of the natural sciences.[28] The relative absence of method in moral judgment, he argues, is compensated by the extent to which, in exercising judgment, we belong to a a tradition. History is not merely an object of study; as what he calls *Wirkungsgeschichte*, it shapes us and works through us in all our activities. He insists, as Aristotle did, that the acquisition of moral judgment requires training in the performance of right action, and that this formation of character can thus emerge only within a historical community in which moral considerations are important.[29]

Although this idea of the dependence of the acquisition of judgment upon training and tradition is scarcely incorrect, it does little, however, to illuminate what the exercise of judgment itself consists in. Indeed, in the way Gadamer uses this idea, it obscures what is so significant about the phenomenon. Whatever may be the conditions for the acquisition of moral judgment, they hardly suffice, in conjunction with moral rules, to determine in what way it is exercised. It cannot be denied, of course, that there exist some connections between how one exercises moral judgment and the circumstances of one's earlier experience and characteristic concerns of the community to which one belongs. But the person of judgment is not one who simply repeats actions that have proven or have been deemed successful in the past. Rather, he is one who can exploit past experience creatively in responding to the novel features that particular situations present. Gadamer's appeal to training and tradition, while capturing an important aspect of moral judgment, cannot suffice to describe what moral judgment is over and above the knowledge of moral rules without covering over what seems so significant about the exercise of judgment – namely, creative insight. Sometimes he recognizes just this point, observing that in the exercise of judgment tradition is always understood differently and innovationally.[30] If this is so, it is plain that the mere fact of participating in a tradition falls short of capturing the nature of judgment. At other times he loses this insight, as in his debate with Habermas. Gadamer appears to believe that to Habermas's idea that reflection can always reconstruct the rules governing some human activity there can only be opposed his conviction that we are always "more being than consciousness," bound up in tradition in ways we can never fully make explicit.[31] Between these two alternatives the very phenomenon of moral judgment becomes lost.

THEORY AND PRACTICE

I believe that the inability of Aristotle, Smith, and Gadamer to give a general account of what the exercise of moral judgment consists in is not lamentable, but exemplary. Although we can understand what kinds of situations call for moral judgment, the kinds of tasks that moral judgment is to accomplish, and the preconditions for its acquisition, there is very little positive we can say in general about the nature of moral judgment itself. We find ourselves providing what are really negative descriptions: The activity of moral judgment goes beyond (while depending upon) what is given in the content of moral rules, characteristic sentiments, and tradition and training. We appear able to say only what judgment is *not*, and not what it *is*. Thus we can use Ryle's distinction to say that judgment is a case of "knowing how" as opposed to "knowing that," but this distinction succeeds in characterizing "knowing how" only in terms of its not having the crucial features of "knowing that."

This inability to arrive at a general theory of judgment should not surprise us, however, if we reflect upon what has become in modern times our ("technical") idea of theoretical understanding. To understand some empirical phenomenon, we believe, consists in discerning the laws to which it is subject. Accordingly, we believe we have an adequate theory of some intentional human practice, if we can reconstruct the rules, both explicit and tacit, that characterize it (if we are committed reductionists, we will look for a nonintentional, e.g., physiological, law-governed redescription of it). The distinctive feature of moral judgment, however, is the way in which (considered as an intentional practice) it transcends the explicit or tacit rules upon which it only partially depends.

Intentional forms of activity that are not thoroughly constituted by reconstructible rules are ones that, given our idea of theoretical understanding, we may be tempted to label to that extent as arbitrary. But if moral judgment is not thoroughly rule-governed, it is not arbitrary either. Judgment certainly involves risk.[32] Yet it does not resemble the flipping of a coin or a decisionistic leap of faith. Judgment we do not exercise blindly, but rather by responding with reasons to the particularity of a given situation. The fact that we are struggling to comprehend is that our perception of these reasons as indeed reasons and the response that they motivate go beyond what the general rules given in advance (as well as characteristic sentiments and training) could alone make of the situation.

If moral judgment lies beyond the limits of theoretical understanding, how has it been possible to discuss moral judgment in this chapter? To this challenge a first reply is that what have proven to be negative characterizations serve nonetheless to cirumscribe from without the phenomenon of moral judgment. But a second, more positive reply is that here (as so often in moral thought) experience should count for more than theoretical ideals. We should not hesitate to say that we know that moral judgment exists and know how to recognize it when it occurs just because it appears not to be a phenomenon constituted by reconstructible rules. We should realize not only that there are limits to *theoretical* understanding , but also that there are other kinds of understanding that are more appropriate for grasping the nature of moral judgment.[33]

Theory can carry us only so far in our attempt to grasp the nature of moral judgment. To go further, we must turn above all to the great works of imaginative literature. D. H. Lawrence wrote that the function of the modern novel, in contrast to philosophy, has been to give us a sense of the individuality of our lives, and individuality is best understood in terms of our ability to interpret the content of general rules in responding to particular situations. Indeed, our capacity for moral judgment thrives on the examples of its exercise that we find presented by the literary imagination.

Chapter 2

The limits of neo-Aristotelianism

In the previous chapter I sought to show the significance of a central Aristotelian concept that modern ethical theories have tended to neglect. In so doing, I have meant to ally myself with neo-Aristotelian tendencies in recent moral thought. But there are limits to my enthusiasm for rehabilitating the Stagirite. These reservations will become most apparent if I discuss how my position differs from that of Alasdair MacIntyre's *After Virtue*, which is one of the most important and influential documents of contemporary neo-Aristotelianism.

MacIntyre believes that the loss of an Aristotelian perspective has led to a moral culture that is fragmented and rootless. "The new dark ages," he writes, "are already upon us." His diagnosis is so unqualifiedly bleak because for him the demise of Aristotelianism has not simply made us insensitive to certain parameters of moral life, such as virtue and judgment, whose importance I have just examined. He claims that it has calamitously stripped us of any objective conception of the end or purpose of human existence, any idea of the good life that morality can subserve. In MacIntyre's view, the recovery of Aristotelian ethics must include Aristotle's conviction that the question, What is human life lived at its best? has a single answer and that our success as moral beings depends upon understanding this answer.

This sort of neo-Aristotelianism is inimical to political liberalism, as MacIntyre well intends it to be. At the heart of the liberal position stand two ideas that I distinguished and discussed in the Preface: *pluralism,* or the idea that there are many viable conceptions of the good life that neither represent different versions of some single, homogeneous good nor fall into any discernible hierarchy; and *toleration,* or the idea that because reasonable persons disagree about the value of various conceptions of the good life, we must learn to live with those who do not share our ideals. Neither pluralism nor toleration makes any sense in the light of a monistic view of the good life about which reasonable people will supposedly agree. On the whole, MacIntyre wishes to reaffirm this feature of Aristotelianism; for the liberal idea that government should remain neutral toward competing conceptions of the good life he has little more than contempt.[1] In this chapter I shall argue that we have no good reason to follow MacIntyre in making this part of Aristotelian ethics our own.

MACINTYRE'S INDICTMENT OF MODERNITY

It is the teleological aspect of Aristotle's ethics that MacIntyre is most concerned to recapture. Aristotle claimed that all men desire happiness or to live a fulfilled life, even if they often disagree about what such a life would consist in. The correctness of attributing even so indeterminate an ultimate end to everyone is open to dispute. But the part of Aristotelian teleology that MacIntyre wishes to oppose to modernity is a belief that is independent of that empirical generalization. Aristotle believed that there is a single, rather determinate answer to the question, what is human life lived at its best? The good life, according to Aristotle, is activity in accord with virtue, which must involve theoretical contemplation and political activity, in that order. I shall discuss later in more detail some of the complexities of Aristotle's conception of the good life. Let us examine first what MacIntyre believes the consequences must be, if as modern pluralists we give up this single and quite determinate view of human flourishing.

Because of its links with Aristotle's philosophy of nature, MacIntyre claims, this teleological view disappeared when Aristotelian physics was rejected at the beginning of modern times. This rejection was a grave misfortune, he believes, because Aristotelian ethics was able to justify moral rules by showing how their observance would lead to the realization of our telos, the attainment of the good life. Once there had been discarded any hope of discerning our telos, however, we were left only with human life as we actually find it and a set of moral rules handed down to us from the past. The possibilities for justifying these rules had been drastically reduced. The price of giving up Aristotle's conception of the good life is ultimately nihilism. Our moral rules are the shards of a lost vision that gave them their point, MacIntyre insists, and so we cannot simply dismiss the force of Nietzsche's demand that we replace our inherited moral code with a radically new one.[2]

According to MacIntyre, the demise of Aristotelian ethics has had three fundamental consequences for modern moral life. First, the disappearance of a conception of the good life that could justify and order various moral rules has led to the occurrence of rationally interminable moral disputes. Without a shared view of our ultimate purpose we often cannot agree about how to decide between rival claims, for we simply invoke different moral rules.[3] Secondly, the absence of a fixed view of the good life to which our individual choices must be subordinated has effectively removed all limits to the scope of individual choice. In liberal societies the government is supposed to remain neutral with respect to different conceptions of the good life, so such societies consist of individualist selves who refuse identification with any contingent circumstances such as character, roles, or institutions. All associations with others and all life-plans have become voluntary.[4] Finally, because moral discourse has therefore become the expression of individual preferences, incapable of rational consensus, practical reason has come to be equated instead with the instrumental reason of bureaucratic institutions, the choice of efficient means to arbitrarily chosen ends. Whatever the mutual antagonism between liberal individualism and bureaucratic impersonality, they are dialectical opposites that thrive off one another.[5]

These theoretical and historical points are scarcely so original as MacIntyre suggests. His diagnosis of the consequences of rejecting Aristotelianism parallels that of other neo-Aristotelians such as Leo Strauss and Hannah Arendt. It also resembles some of the leading ideas of the Frankfurt School. In the *Dialectic of Enlightenment*, Adorno and Horkheimer proclaimed that having repudiated any substantial goal or telos located in the order of nature, the Enlightenment could offer only an instrumental notion of reason that could not rule out the pursuit of the most barbarous ends and that must lead to the bureaucratic domination of men as well as of nature: Sade, they urged, was as much as Kant a representative of the Enlightenment, which is inherently totalitarian.[6] In addition, MacIntyre's antithesis between modern and ancient society rehearses the Romantic notion that premodern societies were organic, fused by a single conception of the good life, whereas modern societies have become fragmented, slipping into anomie. Simplistic dichotomies of this sort do not bear very much scrutiny.[7] MacIntyre has been led to such flimsy historical generalizations, I believe, because of a fundamental misconception about the nature of liberalism. The "individualism" associated with liberalism is not understood by him as a *political* doctrine, according to which goverment should *treat* persons as individuals (i.e., apart from status and ascription), but rather as a general theory of human nature that denies the importance of shared commitments. This misunderstanding of liberalism, the failure to appreciate that by its very nature liberalism must be a philosophy of politics, and not a philosophy of man, is one in which MacIntyre is far from being alone. In later chapters of this book I shall show why and how this misunderstanding is to be avoided. Here I want to examine more closely why MacIntyre believes that giving up what he thinks is most distinctive of Aristotelian ethics – the idea that morality promotes the good life – has fatal theoretical consequences.

Nowhere does MacIntyre find a clearer expression of the rejection of Aristotelianism than in what he understands as the Enlightenment project of providing an autonomous foundation of morality.[8] This project was the attempt to give the moral rules inherited from the preceding culture a systematic justification that would not appeal to any extramoral (e.g., metaphysical or theological) views about the end or purpose of human existence. The hope of the Enlightenment was to develop a conception of morality independently of a religious world picture. MacIntyre believes that an autonomous justification of moral beliefs must select some basic feature of human nature as it exists and show that any being with this feature would come to accept those beliefs. According to MacIntyre, there were three basic ways of carrying out this project, associated with who he believes are the three greatest moral thinkers of the eighteenth century – Hume, Kant, and Bentham. None of the ways, he thinks, could possibly succeed.

Let me follow through what MacIntyre has to say about each of these alternatives. Hume sought to base the accepted moral rules upon our desires and sentiments. But he was necessarily selective about which desires and sentiments to place at the foundation of morality, and so he would have been at a loss, MacIntyre claims, before someone (such as Rameau's nephew, described by Diderot) who might choose a different set, in fact antagonistic to existing morality. Moreover, Hume himself recognized, according to MacIntyre, that desires and sentiments are typically too variable in intensity to support a steady sense of obligation, and so he resorted to the idea of "sympathy" – simply a "philosophical fiction," says MacIntyre, concocted to be at once sentimental and constant. Kant, on the other hand, tried to rescue the accepted moral rules from these difficulties by connecting them with certain general features of reason. Against this position MacIntyre repeats two very familiar objections:

1. The principle of universalizability does not form a sufficient condition for a maxim being moral because there are universalizable maxims that are immoral.

2. This principle, while perhaps a distinctive feature of reason, cannot justify Kant's morally more substantial principle that persons are to be treated not merely as means but also as ends.

To more recent Kantian attempts to found morality upon the abstract idea of rational agency (here MacIntyre refers to Gewirth and Rawls), he objects that the theories of rights at which they arrive cannot work since the notion of a right is vacuous when unrelated to concrete social institutions.[9] Nor, finally, has utilitarianism (from Bentham to today) fared any better, in MacIntyre's view. Recognizing Kantianism's inability to secure specific moral rules on the basis only of abstract ideas of rational agency, utilitarians have tried to set up a new teleological perspective. But, he claims, either the conception of happiness to which moral rules are to be subordinated is too restrictive and suffocating, as in Bentham, or it becomes so broad and all-encompassing, as in Mill, that it turns useless. Thus he concludes that the fundamental concepts of utilitarianism, like those of Kantianism and Humeanism, are "pseudo-concepts," so vacuous or ambiguous that in modern times moral debate has become rationally interminable and moral beliefs express only individual preferences.[10] Emotivism may be a poor theory of the meaning of moral concepts, but it captures, he believes, the way we now use them.[11]

THE OBJECTIVITY AND AUTONOMY OF MORALS

There is a lot to be criticized in this potted history of modern moral thought. It does not rise much above the sort of simplification characteristic of MacIntyre's historical generalizations. However, instead of pointing out the various inaccuracies of this account, I want to examine its underlying philosophical assumptions.

MacIntyre's basic idea seems to be that without some conception of the good life that includes more than morality itself and that morality can be seen to promote, our moral experience must fall into disarray. Without such a foundation, moral beliefs will lack any plausible claim to objectivity, and morality must become the site of rationally unsettlable conflicts. Perhaps the first thing to notice is that these two supposed consequences of making morality autonomous could well be logically distinct. Depending on how the notion of "objectivity" is understood, two moral principles might both be "objective," in any case more than a matter of mere "individual preference," and yet we might not have a way of rationally settling conflicts that arise between the directives they yield in particular circumstances. This, I believe, can in fact be the case, and MacIntyre himself ultimately believes so as well. But before saying more about this problem, I want to show why MacIntyre is wrong to associate the idea of the autonomy of morality with a collapse of objectivity.

I shall begin with what I consider MacIntyre's "master argument" for why the idea of the autonomy of morals must undermine their objectivity. He claims that the traditional theory of the virtues included three components: "untutored human nature as it happens to be, human nature as it could be if it realized its telos, and the precepts of rational ethics as the means for the transition from one to the other."[12] Enlightenment culture jettisoned a conception of the human telos; but its effort to derive the moral rules simply from human nature as it happens to be was bound to fail, for human beings are so diverse and anyway inclined to disobey those rules. Thus moral claims lack the means for objectivity in Enlightenment culture, where by objectivity is meant that moral statements "can be called true or false in precisely the way in which all other factual statements can be so called."[13]

I called this MacIntyre's master argument not because I think it is particularly good, but rather because I think it is about the only systematic argument that he has, and it is the argument that he shares with other neo-Aristotelians such as Strauss and Arendt.

One of its erroneous assumptions is that the *contextual* justification of moral beliefs cannot secure their objectivity. For MacIntyre the justification of a moral claim by appealing to various nonmoral facts *and to other moral beliefs* that we already hold and that are not, in this context, subject to question amounts apparently to no proper justification at all. His master argument supposes that we can ensure the objectivity of some moral belief, not if we simply justify it contextually by reference to others held constant, but only if all our moral beliefs can be justified en masse, only if we can show that *as a whole* they get us from untutored human nature to some extramoral telos. So, in fact, MacIntyre's argument is epistemological foundationalism carried over to the realm of morality.

Now contextualism – the view that a disputed belief is sufficiently justified if justified by appeal to other beliefs not challenged by the particular dispute – is a reasonable and increasingly accepted epistemology for science.[14] And yet setting aside the hope of grounding our scientific beliefs upon unshakable foundations, altogether immune to revision, need not lead us to impugn the objectivity of science. Why then should the objectivity of morals be in question, just because morality is seen as autonomous? To the extent that moral beliefs are contextually justifiable, they can be called true or false in just the way that factual scientific beliefs are, and so they can lay claim to objectivity in precisely the sense that MacIntyre intends.

It cannot be denied, I think, that on one point MacIntyre is right: The scientistic view that scientific knowledge is the only knowledge we possess is a powerful and regrettable current in our culture. But the economical way to counter this subjectivization of morals lies, not in recovering an ideal of the good life to which morality can be viewed as a means, but instead in recognizing that scientism rests on epistemological error; it invokes either a false epistemology (foundationalism) or a double standard by making demands of morality it does not make of science. MacIntyre himself appears to make the latter mistake, and so he remains part of the problem, not of the solution.[15]

There is a second important mistake in MacIntyre's master argument. It mislocates the real difference between Aristotelian and modern ideas about the relation between morality and the good life. The Enlightenment's aim was to work out a conception of morality independently of a religious world view. In this regard the Enlightenment's main target was not Aristotelianism, but rather certain traditions of Christian ethics. As a matter of fact, Aristotelian ethics shares just that autonomous conception of morality that MacIntyre regards as distinctive of the Enlightenment. Aristotle did not think of virtue as a "means" for getting untutored human nature to some *third* component that is our telos, but instead understood the exercise of virtue as what the good life *consists in*. The tripartite scheme figuring in MacIntyre's master argument corresponds rather to a particular theological view, namely that in morality lies the route to salvation, as well as to certain egoistic views that were current in the seventeenth and eighteenth cenuturies but that the greatest Enlightenment moralists combatted.[16]

All this should become clear once we recognize that the autonomy of morality, properly understood, is the idea that we attain our real humanity only in and through morality. The autonomy of morality does not imply, as MacIntyre suggests, that we must blindly perform duty for duty's sake, without regard to what that makes of us. This view is a caricature of Kant's position; the fact that Kant reserved the *term* "happiness" for a part of the good life that is distinct from moral action should not obscure the fact that for him only morality allows us to apprehend what gives human existence its greatest value, because only morality allows us to become *worthy* of happiness. For Kant as for the other great modern moralists, morality is a domain of value that is *sui generis*: It makes accessible for the first time possibilities of human fulfillment whose value we cannot grasp outside morality itself.

The Enlightenment was a period containing many different tendencies, not all of them friendly to this idea that morality is an autonomous source of value. But three of the greatest moral thinkers of that age – Butler, Rousseau, and Kant – articulated this idea for modern times. It is a striking fact that despite all their differences, they even chose the same way of putting this idea. A man becomes fully human only when, instead of remaining subject to given needs and desires, he shapes his conduct by a law he gives himself, and morality is not only one form of such self-legislation, but also a necessary one for our full humanity.[17] This does not mean (nor did it mean for Butler, Rousseau, or Kant) that moral rules are valid simply because we impose them upon ourselves. Nor must this idea of the self-legislation of morality be connected, as it was in Kant but not in Butler, with the idea of self-determination, that is, with the idea of an empirically unconditioned interest in morality.[18] Becoming a moral agent depends upon social conditions of training and practice that we do not control ourselves. But however we understand what makes moral rules valid, and whatever we think about how we acquire our interest in morality, we can still hold onto what these three moralists believed in common about what it is to *be* a moral agent. In general, our humanity requires that we do not lead our lives as merely a sequence of desires satisfied or disappointed, but rather that we shape and interpret our activities and experiences in terms of over-arching rules and purposes; only in this way do peculiarly human values and significances become intelligible and accessible. Morality itself, they argued, is the most important of these humanizing patterns in which we organize our life, and one that brings with it specific forms of fulfillment and satisfaction.

Moreover, contrary to MacIntyre, this idea that morality has intrinsic worth is not a peculiarly modern one, lying instead at the very heart of Aristotle's ethics. Indeed, we may think of those modern moralists as recovering the ancient sense that morality is an autonomous source of value, which modern partisans of egoistic hedonism (such as Hobbes and Helvétius) had rejected, in a sort of unholy alliance with theologians who also instrumentalized morality. When Aristotle argued that happiness or the good life is life lived in accordance with virtue (the fact that this includes moral and intellectual virtue shall be taken up shortly), he did not think of happiness as a third component *in addition to* the exercise of virtue, to which the latter is a means. Rather, happiness *consists in* the exercise of virtue. Aristotle did claim, of course, that we should choose the life of virtue *because* thereby we attain the fulfilled life that makes us truly human; this fact he expressed by saying that we choose virtue partly for itself and partly for the sake of our happiness.[19] Yet far from corresponding to MacIntyre's tripartite scheme, this locution indicates that the virtuous life is indeed of intrinsic value, indeed a form of life chosen for its own sake, and only *thereby* a form of life through which we attain true happiness. In other words, Aristotle believed that the fulfilled life is not to be had if we aim simply at it, regarding virtue as a means; we must value the virtuous life for its own sake, for only so does our highest happiness, which is specific to it, become intelligible and appreciable. Aristotle, too, believed (as is clear from the beginning of I.2 in the *Eudemian Ethics*) that happiness or the fulfillment of our humanity acquires its significance only in and through a general view of the good life that we impose upon our conduct and experience.

Although there are certainly important differences between Aristotle and modern moralists such as Butler, Rousseau, and Kant, those differences do not include the question of the autonomy of morality. For Aristotle, too, virtue is its own reward. There is no end distinct from the virtuous life to which he considered that life a means. He certainly did not appeal to a general teleology of nature to pick out such an independent end. Although it is widely held that Aristotle's view of the proper human end depended upon his teleological metaphysics, the textual evidence for this dependence is quite slender.²⁰ There is only the discussion of man's function in *Nicomachean Ethics* I.7, and in any case this passage characterizes that function as a life lived in accordance with virtue; it does not call into question the autonomy of virtue. So if Aristotelian ethics lost some of its prestige in the seventeenth and eighteenth centuries, this was probably not because of a general distrust of metaphysical teleology and a recourse to the idea of the autonomy of morality, as MacIntyre claims. The view that virtue is an autonomous source of value is already there in Aristotle's thought, and whatever their views about metaphysical teleology, those three modern moralists agreed with Aristotle that in the moral life man first becomes fully human, realizing his "function."

In his own discussion of Aristotelian ethics, as opposed to the unflattering contrast he draws between it and modern ethics, MacIntyre seems to acknowledge that for Aristotle, too, virtue is an autonomous source of value. Virtue, MacIntyre says, is a means "internal" to our telos. A means is internal "when the end cannot be adequately characterized independently of a characterization of the means," so that the exercise of the virtues is a "necessary and central part" of human life lived at its best.²¹ This formulation fits Aristotle's idea that happiness consists in the exercise of the virtues, but it is needlessly roundabout. Our terminology of means and end naturally suggests that a means has only instrumental value. Since this is precisely what Aristotle wanted to deny about virtue, we do better to say that the exercise of virtue is that in which happiness consists, rather than concoct the hybrid notion of an "internal means."

So far I have skirted an important feature of Aristotle's definition of happiness – a life lived in accordance with virtue – from which MacIntyre, too, has turned his attention. By "virtue" Aristotle meant the intellectual virtues as well as the strictly moral ones; moreover, at least in Book X of the *Nicomachean Ethics*, he claimed that the exercise of the intellectual virtues, above all in the activity of theoretical contemplation, represents the highest form of human happiness, because in it we become like the gods. (We cannot attain such a state permanently, Aristotle conceded, so our feasible ideal must be a life of both intellectual and moral virtue; but we should strive as much as possible to approach the divine life of intellect alone.) This shows first of all that, contrary to MacIntyre, Aristotle's ethics contains individualistic strands as unqualified as anything to be found in modern thought: Aristotle contended that life lived at its best will be lived apart from society.[22] It should not be thought, however, that as a result he must have considered morality as having only the instrumental value of making contemplation possible. Morality constitutes a "secondary" form of happiness, he wrote in *Nicomachean Ethics* X.8, not a means toward the primary form.

Most importantly, we come here to the real point at which Aristotelian and modern ethics disagree about the relation of morality to the good life. Aristotle held a *monistic* view of human fulfillment, maintaining that there is a thoroughgoing hierarchy among conceptions of the good life. The best life is that of theoretical contemplation, the second best that of political activity in which the moral virtues are best exercised.[23] Modern thinkers have generally been reluctant to follow in Aristotle's path of asserting that any single form of life represents the best for man. Theory, as practiced in the sciences, now seems to have little to do with "contemplation." However, their main reason for not exalting it as the best life is not this, but rather their belief that other forms of life involve equally valuable human goods. Similarly, even if the image of the polis has not lost its charm for all modern moral thinkers (Rousseau is one of the best examples), most have found no reason to attribute to politics, in contrast to other areas of the social world, any greater capacity for realizing our humanity.

Now the reason why Aristotle had this monistic view of the good life, attributing to politics this special role in realizing our humanity, is precisely his belief that in political activity the moral virtues are best exercised. This is the belief that modern moralists have generally rejected in the name of pluralism and toleration. This rejection should not be construed (as it has sometimes been) to mean that the nonpolitical areas of social life must necessarily succeed in fostering the moral life, nor that the political realm cannot serve this function under any conditions. Rather, the modern view has been that the political life harbors no essentially greater attraction to the moral life than does the religious life, or the economic life, or the family, and so on, or at the very least that reasonable people can disagree about which form of life is thus superior (to insist upon this fact has been one central aim of the modern distinction between the "state" and "society").

Here lies the most important reason why modern moralists have proven more open to the pluralism of viable conceptions of the good life and to the toleration of disagreement about them. Here is also the reason why in modern ethics the notion of the good life has expanded to include more than just the morality that is binding upon everyone (and not necessarily to include *theoria*). If many different forms of life provide basically equal opportunities for the exercise of morality, or if reasonable people disagree about their worth in this regard, then the ways in which these forms of life differ will figure as areas of a conception of the good life that go beyond universalistic morality itself. In other words, the notion of a good life will in general come to include two components – a universally binding morality and a plurality of forms of fulfillment, which Kant, for example, termed "happiness." Indeed, Kant's own notion of the good life, or what he called the summum bonum, offers one of the best known articulations of this modern idea.[24] Thus, both the belief that there are many different forms of life equally favorable to universalistic morality as well as the recognition that there exists reasonable disagreement about their value, have given a complexity to the idea of the good life that is absent from Aristotle's thought. This is the sense in which henceforth I shall refer to the modern acceptance of the variety and indomitable controversiality of ideals of the good life.

Aristotle's monism is what MacIntyre seems most eager to

rehabilitate, at least when he is railing against modern pluralism. So far we have seen that he fails to grasp what is at
stake if we do not share such a monistic view of the good
life. The objectivity, as well as the autonomy, of morals will
remain untouched. What must change is the relation between
the ideas of morality and the good life.

A MODERNIST MALGRÉ LUI

I want to turn now to a peculiar but also salutary feature of
MacIntyre's book. It is the way he repeatedly undercuts the
very indictments of modernity he seems most concerned to
stand by. The gravest mistake of modern ethics, he claims,
lies in having surrendered Aristotle's view that human life
has a telos or objective purpose. As a result of this development, there has arisen the modern doctrine of pluralism,
the view that the idea of the good life can be variously in-
terpreted by reasonable people, and morality itself has
become the locus of rationally interminable disputes. Mac-
Intyre's attacks upon modernity urge unambiguously that
these are bad things. And yet his own efforts to work out a
conception of our telos and his own estimation of the possibilities of reasoned moral agreement turn him toward just
the positions he seems so much to detest.

MacIntyre wants to rehabilitate the concepts of virtue and
the good life by disconnecting them from Aristotle's "metaphysical biology" and linking them with the ideas of a practice and of the unity of a life.[25] He defines a practice as a
cooperative human activity having shared standards of ex-
cellence that determine a form of success that is *intrinsically*
related to the activity involved. Such "internal goods" (success in game-playing, or in intellectual endeavors, or in family life) cannot be characterized except in relation to the
activities constituting the practice; and it is these activities
that are to be understood as the exercise of a particular virtue.
Practices are to be distinguished from "institutions," according to MacIntyre, because the latter are forms of activity

geared toward "external goods" such as money, power, and status.[26] External goods constitute resources, whose value lies not in how we acquired them but rather in what we can do with them.

Practices so defined, however, can often turn out to be at odds with one another. MacIntyre himself acknowledges that there can thus be conflicts between different conceptions of the good life, embodied in different practices. In order to avoid any slippage toward pluralism, he therefore falls back upon the idea that we have a telos or end that transcends specific practices, an overarching purpose that consists in the unity of a good life.[27] When forced at last to give some content to the idea of the good life that we all can share, however, MacIntyre can suggest only that it "is the life spent in seeking for the good life for man."[28] So tentative a conclusion belongs to a pluralistic perspective. It plainly allows that life lived at its best will be differently but reasonably construed by different individuals and groups. So the inconsistency between MacIntyre's idea of the good life and his hankering after Aristotelian monism bears testimony to what must be his own deep-seated allegiance to modernity.

A similar inconsistency figures in MacIntyre's attitude toward the second sign of disorder that he claims to find in our moral culture: the presence of moral conflicts that seem to defy rational solution.

Aristotle gives no evidence of recognizing that morality could be the site of rationally interminable conflicts. This does not mean that, like Kant or Bentham, he conceived of the moral agent as provided with an effective decision procedure, consisting of a set of fully determinate moral rules, that would yield an answer for every moral problem. Judgment played an indispensable role in Aristotle's idea of moral decision making. So in this sense he was skeptical of one of the simplistic ambitions of systematic moral theory. But this did not prevent him from apparently sharing another of them; namely, that conflicts between what our moral beliefs require of us in particular situations indicate a lack of knowledge (including the "know-how" embodied in our capacity for judgment) on our part, and not a heterogeneity of the moral order itself.[29]

I do not believe that this hope is well founded. No mature view of morality can fail to acknowledge the existence of rationally unsettlable moral conflicts. Pluralism is a truth, not only about conceptions of the good life, but also about that dimension of the good life that is morality itself.

In Chapter 6 I shall show in some detail why this is so. I want to conclude the present chapter by pointing out that MacIntyre himself, despite his condemnation of modernity for accepting a pluralism in morals, embraces it as well.

The Greeks of classical times were sensitive, he says, both to the potential for moral conflict within the preclassical, heroic ethic (as in the *Oresteia*) and to the moral conflicts between their heroic traditions and the different social context of the polis (as in the *Antigone*). So moral conflict figured in classical society as well as in modern society. Moreover, MacIntyre also believes that often such conflicts did not appear to admit of rational solution to the more perceptive such as Aeschylus or Sophocles. In fact, he criticizes Aristotle, Plato, and Aquinas for thinking that the rational and good man will not encounter irresolvable moral conflict. And he praises the Greek tragedians for handling such conflicts, not by argument but rather by a deus ex machina, where "the divine verdict always ends rather than resolves the conflict."[30] Contrary to what the reader might first expect, the hero of his book turns out to be not Aristotle but Sophocles, precisely because Sophocles recognized that there are rationally interminable moral conflicts.

If all this is so, MacIntyre's contrast between the fragmentation of modernity and the more wholesome tradition of antiquity apparently comes to naught. Desperately shifting his ground, he asserts that unlike modern moralists (Weber, Berlin) who also believe in the inevitability of moral conflicts, Sophocles understood such conflicts as *tragic*: The alternative that we do not choose still has a claim on us and so our choice is accompanied by regret.[31] But this maneuver could not be more unfair. Weber had nothing if not a tragic awareness of the other values that modern society has neglected or forsaken in rationalizing world views and social relations. His pluralism, like Berlin's, did not question the objectivity of moral value, but rather its homogeneity, or the idea that there can be a systematic moral theory that will provide a way of settling all moral disputes without denying some of our deepest moral commitments. Precisely because objectivity does not entail homogeneity, such moralists can recognize that a loss of moral value, and so regret, can accompany our moral choices.[32] Thus, MacIntyre invokes a double standard when contrasting modern and premodern moral thought. Irresolvable moral conflict leads the Supreme Court, he complains, to function as "a trucekeeping body . . . negotiating its way through an impasse of conflict."[33] But would things be any better if we substituted a deus ex machina for the Supreme Court? Rational argument, if not always rational consensus, plays a considerable role in the Court's deliberations. And unlike the gods, judges are mortal, replaceable by others who may turn out better.

In conclusion we should recognize that the insights of Aristotle's ethics are sharply limited. He saw clearly the importance of certain aspects of the moral life that modern ethics has too often ignored. But his views of the good life and of morality itself reveal a narrowness we should not feel compelled to imitate. The good and the right contain dimensions of complexity of which he apparently had no idea. There is no doubt that from his point of view a culture such as ours, which has largely accepted these complexities, must appear "rootless" and "fragmented." But in this case such terms show only the simplistic expectations with which one is approaching the subject. The terminology of wholes, parts, and fragments is one that ultimately we have inherited from Aristotle himself; but here, as so often elsewhere, it proves not only unhelpful, but positively misleading.[34]

Once relaxed from his philippics against modernity, MacIntyre seems to share this assessment. He, too, acknowledges that we must not try to return to Aristotle's excessive desire for unity. He, too, is a pluralist, *malgré lui*.

Chapter 3

Liberalism and the neutrality of the state

IN PRAISE OF BUREAUCRACY

I argued in Chapter 1 that by neglecting the phenomenon of judgment, modern ethics has not faced up to the complexity of the phenomena with which it should be concerned. We must learn to take more seriously Aristotle's remark that in ethics we should tailor our desire for system to what the subject matter permits.[1]

There are circumstances, nonetheless, where heeding this complexity would be misplaced. In some cases decision making in accordance with a system of rules that yields single directives in almost every case, but that corresponds only *grosso modo* to our considered moral judgments, may outweigh a more faithfully nuanced appreciation of the way things are. Most of all this is true of the political realm. There system can prove more desirable than sensitivity for a very important reason. Whenever the government acts according to publicly known statutes and laws that allow little room for conflicting directives, this gives its actions a *predictability* that can be invaluable for those who must make decisions in other areas of society, or in other branches of government. An investment banker will often be more interested in knowing precisely what the government's central bank will do about the money supply than in knowing merely that, whatever the government's decisions here, they will be morally correct. Indeed, we might even say that one of the *moral* demands that we make of government is that it act predictably. Its great concentration of power is tolerable only if, foreseeing how this power will be exercised, we can plan our own lives accordingly and take the necessary precautions.[2] Thus, we might be willing to put up with a government whose decisions lack the sensitivity we prize in our private lives, so long as we thereby secure what can be the greater value of knowing in advance what the government will do.

A failure to appreciate this point seems to me to undermine Oakeshott's praise of political elites who govern by uncodified know-how, by judgment and awareness of moral complexities, instead of public statutes.[3] Naturally we value practical wisdom above bureaucratic efficiency when we consider what we want to be as persons. I showed why this is so in my earlier chapter on judgment. But we must make different demands of governments than we make of individuals, because of the very different degrees to which they can affect our lives. As Adam Smith observed, we should require of the political virtue of justice a precision and determinacy of rules that we do not expect of other virtues.

Political systems lacking a highly developed bureaucratic apparatus, for example the Greek polis, may prove to be arenas for a broader and more subtle exercise of virtue than anything we can witness in modern Western political life. But for this they pay a very high price; namely, far less freedom to pursue other activities independently of political control. "Ancient liberty" is too narrow for modern souls who recognize that politics is just one among a plurality of reasonable ideals of the good life. To the extent that a state's decisions are less predictable, institutions in the rest of society are less able to plan and control their own activities. Thus, to a greater predictability in government corresponds a greater freedom of the other spheres of social life.[4].

This is the sense in which modern societies have displaced politics from the role of center that it enjoyed at least in the Greek ideal of the polis (whatever the extent of its realization in ancient Greece). Government has remained the greatest concentration of power in society, but other areas of society are no longer so directly subordinate to it as before. Bureaucracy has thus become a condition of freedom. It permits a significant and liberating separation of the public and the private.

The distinction between the public and the private is one that has been variously drawn, and often for polemical purposes having little to do with reality. I shall understand it as picking out different areas of social life: The public has to do with what belongs within the political system, whereas the private covers whatever belongs outside it. Nothing should automatically be assumed about the motives or goals characteristic of these two realms. Most importantly, the private, or the nonpolitical, need not consist chiefly in self-interested activities, blind to any greater good, as some traditions of political thought, especially those inimical to liberalism, have suggested. The private is a domain where morality can flourish as well.

Indeed, the preceding remarks indicate that one complexity of moral experience is more to be appreciated in the private than in the public domain. The political value of predictability is considerable enough that to a certain degree we are willing to forego having the decisions of government display all the subtlety that we expect of the truly virtuous and morally wise. This is one feature, therefore, by which the public and the private are differentiated. But it is not the only one.

WHAT IS NEUTRALITY?

However important predictability may be as a political value, and however much its bureaucratic institutionalization may promote private freedom, it does not form the central ideal of the modern liberal state. Without predictability no liberal state can properly function. But the specific way in which it distinguishes the public from the private is not the feature most characteristic of political liberalism. Instead, the distinctive liberal notion is that of the neutrality of the state. Neutrality of the state ensures a large measure of predictability, but its ultimate rationale lies elsewhere. It grows directly out of what I described in the previous chapter as one of the principal defects of Aristotelian ethics.

The ideal of neutrality can best be understood as a response to the variety of conceptions of the good life. In modern times we have come to recognize a multiplicity of ways in which a fulfilled life can be lived, without any perceptible hierarchy among them. And we have also been forced to acknowledge that even where we do believe that we have discerned the superiority of some ways of life to others, reasonable people may often not share our view. Pluralism and reasonable disagreement have become for modern thought ineliminable features of the idea of the good life. Political liberalism has been the doctrine that consequently the state should be neutral. The state should not seek to promote any particular conception of the good life because of its presumed *intrinsic* superiority – that is, because it is supposedly a *truer* conception. (A liberal state may naturally restrict certain ideals for *extrinsic* reasons because, for example, they threaten the lives of others.)

One of the most important questions of liberal theory concerns the precise way in which pluralism and disagreement should be seen as justifying the neutrality of the state. But before looking at this question, I want first to explain a little more carefully just what such neutrality means.

It is a general truth that what the state does, the decisions it makes and the policies it pursues, will generally benefit some people more than others, and so some conceptions of the good life will fare better than others. This, I believe, is unavoidable. At the very least, those who desire a life of theft will find it rough going. And to take a more serious example, ways of life that depend upon close and exclusive bonds of language and culture – the French in Canada or the Bretons in France – may lose, within a liberal society also tolerating quite different and more open ways of life, some of the authority and cohesion that they would have if they formed complete societies unto themselves. Ideals of the good life that are open in principle to all, whatever one's cultural in-

43

heritance (e.g., professional ideals), may well prove stronger under a liberal state. There is no getting around the fact that goods are not all fully compatible, that gains generally entail losses.

But all of this does not impugn the neutrality of the liberal state. Its neutrality is not meant to be one of *outcome*, but rather one of *procedure*.[5] That is, political neutrality consists in a constraint on what factors can be invoked to justify a political decision. Such a decision can count as neutral only if it can be justified without appealing to the presumed intrinsic superiority of any particular conception of the good life. So long as a government conforms its decisions to this constraint, therefore, it will be acting neutrally. There is no independently describable condition of society to be called "neutral" that the ideal of political neutrality requires a government promote or maintain.

Neutrality understood procedurally leaves open to a large extent the *goals* that the liberal state ought to pursue. Of course, some ends (e.g., the establishment of a state religion) are impermissible, because there can be no neutrally justifiable decision to pursue them. But any goals for whose pursuit there exists a neutral justification are ones that a liberal state may pursue. I do not think that the protection of life and property are the only goals that will satisfy this condition. The ideal of neutrality would not prevent a state from undertaking to ensure a particular pattern of wealth distribution, so long as the desirability of this pattern does not presuppose the superiority of some views of human flourishing over others held in society. (As I shall argue later, Rawls's original position is best understood as a position of neutrality, so one might think here of his argument for the difference principle.) So a neutral state need not necessarily be a "minimal state." Nineteenth-century liberals who demanded a minimal "nightwatchman" state (the Manchester school, for example) may have had many reasons – some intellectually responsible, some not – for this view, but their best reason was the idea that the free market is the most efficient and neutral means of producing and distributing wealth and resources. A contemporary liberal who desires a more active interventionist role for the state is best understood as still sharing their ideal of liberal neutrality, but as disagreeing with them about the nature of the free market.

The theoretical possibility that a liberal state can be one that intervenes in social life (subject to the constraint of neutrality) is also, of course, a historical fact. The development of liberalism over the past century has involved *both* an increase in individual freedom and an increase in state power – and this should be paradoxical only to those who believe that power is a zero-sum game.[6] This state intervention has not been equal, however, in all areas of social life: The liberal state has undertaken to manage the economy and redistribute wealth, but it has not interfered with the membership rules of churches, for example. How can the ideal of neutrality explain this fact?

In order to answer this question, I must begin by emphasizing that for the liberal, neutrality is a *political* ideal. The state's policies and decisions must be neutrally justifiable, but the liberal does not require that other institutions in society operate in the same spirit. Churches and firms, for example, may pursue goals (salvation, profits) that they assume to be ideals intrinsically superior to others. In other words, neutrality as a political ideal governs the *public* relations between persons and the state, and not the *private* relations between persons and other institutions. This is a very important feature of liberalism, and in Chapter 5 I shall discuss how antiliberal critics have generally failed to appreciate it. But here I am using this point to a different purpose. How can a neutral state justifiably treat firms and churches differently, taxing firms for the purposes of income redistribution and imposing on them fair hiring procedures, while allowing churches to maintain restrictive membership rules?

The answer lies in the fact that economic efficiency has been a neutrally justifiable goal in modern Western societies, while personal salvation has not been one. To promote economic efficiency (in abstraction from how this may conflict with other goals) does not suppose the intrinsic superiority

45

of some ideals of the good life over others held in these societies. With the recognition that the free market is not adequately efficient, the liberal state could come justifiably to intervene in economic activity. Since, however, the state must regulate the distribution of wealth, in order to enhance efficiency, it should not allow distribution to be determined on nonneutral grounds. It cannot justifiably assume that the interests of the wealthy are intrinsically superior to those of the poor.

This seems to me the way in which liberals ought to think about the justifiability of progessive income taxation and welfare legislation. I am not claiming that this form of justification was the most prominent in the recent rise of liberal state intervention; nor do I believe that all aspects of that intervention can be so justified or that all justifiable forms of such intervention have been tried. Specific questions of this sort are not my concern here. What I wish to emphasize is the general reason why a liberal state could intervene in one area of social life and not in another. It is not that the area of intervention does not itself exemplify neutrality. For a liberal, neutrality is a political, not a general social ideal. The liberal state can intervene in an area of social life only if the state has a neutrally justifiable goal that requires that intervention, and only to the extent required by its pursuit of that goal can it justifiably institutionalize neutrality in that area.

Liberalism as a political doctrine has generally been associated with the ideal of freedom. I think that this has been a mixed blessing because of all the different things that "freedom" can mean. One distinct advantage of making neutrality the primary ideal of liberalism is that it explains what freedom has generally meant for the political liberal. By denying the state any right to foster or implement any conception of the good life that some people reject, neutrality emphasizes the equal freedom that all persons should have to pursue their conception of the good life. This fact shows not only how the liberal state will differ from states whose ambition it is to promote some conception of the good life, but also that, for the purposes of liberal political theory, "freedom" has a sharply circumscribed sense. It covers only the right of the person not to face neutrally unjustifiable interference by the state. It conforms, in other words, to what Isaiah Berlin has called the "negative" conception of freedom, that we find in the writing of classical liberals such as Locke, Kant, Constant, Tocqueville, and Mill. Now the crucial point to recognize is that liberals need regard negative freedom only as a *political* ideal. They need not deny that as an ideal for the good life, freedom should mean more than the absence of a certain sort of governmental interference; positively, freedom must include, perhaps, self-realization or the availability of "meaningful" choices. However, just as ideals of the good life are a permanent object of dispute, so too are more substantial ideals of freedom, and so it cannot be the concern of the state to promote these. Berlin himself made it fairly clear that negative liberty is a political ideal and need not exhaust everything we mean by freedom, inasmuch as he refused to deny that positive liberty is also a value. The subsequent criticisms of Berlin's work, however, have largely lost any sense of the need to determine what ought to be politically relevant in our manifold idea of freedom.[7]

There remains one last but important observation that I must make about the liberal ideal of political neutrality. It would be misunderstood, if it were thought to minimize the significant role that public discussion (or "Öffentlichkeit") should play in a liberal political culture.[8] In particular, the ideal of political neutrality does not deny that such discussion should encompass not only determining what are the probable consequences of alternative decisions and whether certain decisions can be neutrally justified, but also clarifying one's notion of the good life and trying to convince others of the superiority of various aspects of one's view of human flourishing. This ideal demands only that so long as some view about the good life remains disputed, no decision of the state can be justified on the basis of its supposed intrinsic superiority or inferiority.

NEUTRALITY AND CLASSICAL UTILITARIANISM

Liberals have not always grasped the degree of impartiality that the ideal of procedural neutrality requires. Classical utilitarianism offers a fine example of how a lack of neutrality, a commitment to some disputed view about the good life, may lie concealed in what appears to be a purely formal principle. Utilitarians from Bentham to Sidgwick believed that in order to steer a neutral course among competing ideals, government must aim at the greatest net balance of pleasure or (more neutrally) satisfaction of all the desires involved. The difficulty is that the greatest-happiness principle, under either formulation, harbored a controversial conception of human good. Classical utilitarians held that the only thing ultimately good, and so the standard along which competing ideals are to be "neutrally" weighed, is a certain sort of *experience* – pleasure or satisfaction. It may be true that some people will understand the best life as simply one in which pleasure is preponderant over pain, or as one in which there obtains the greatest net satisfaction of one's desires. But many will not believe this to be the best life.

The utilitarians were not without arguments to show that this is how reasonable people should think of human good. Sidgwick's argument is a typical one.[9] From the fact (so he claimed) that we could not value something as good unless we had the consciousness of its being desirable, he inferred that its goodness consists in the consciousness of its desirableness. This sort of consciousness or experience could then provide (especially if the desirable could be proven equivalent to the pleasurable, as Sidgwick also believed) a common basis on which various goods could be compared and aggregated – for a single individual and across numerous individuals – as the utilitarian principle required. By virtue of demanding the maximization of this common denominator of whatever is held to be good, utilitarians would remain neutral among different views of the good life.

The fundamental error of this argument lies not so much in the equation between the desirable and the pleasurable, as in the inference that paves the way for it, the inference identifying what is held to be good with certain experiences. Even if it is universally true that to attain what one thinks good entails experiencing the satisfaction of desire (and even this is not certain, unless perhaps the notion of "satisfaction" has been rendered so trivial that the utilitarian can make sense of our conviction that it is better to be a Socrates un-satisfied than a pig satisfied), we still need not believe that what we value, and the extent to which we value it, lies in the magnitude, in the intensity and duration, of the experience. What is held to be good may be such that attaining it must result in our having a certain sort of experience; but Sidgwick erred in supposing that the goodness of our goal necessarily consists in our having that sort of experience. On the contrary, the satisfaction that we have in something held to be good (e.g., the correct performance of a Bach chorale, by contrast with eating a tasty meal) often depends precisely upon our believing that we have actually *done* something and not just *experienced* something. To be a good pianist is not simply to have all the mental states or experiences that a good pianist has. So Sidgwick, like other classical utilitarians, was wrong to think that states of mind or experiences are the only things reasonable people may hold to be ultimately good.

Classical utilitarianism fails to be neutral, therefore, because it subscribes to a subjectivistic conception of the good and thus of the good life that many will reasonably not share. For much that is good is not a matter of our experiences, but rather of what we do; and such nonexperiential goods can often be constitutive of some ideal of the good life. The utilitarian principle would force many to understand the value of what they pursue in a manner alien to what makes it of value to them.

There is, I think, an important lesson to be learned from the classical utilitarians' failure. They adopted what may well be a wrong strategy for arriving at a position neutral with respect to different conceptions of the human good. They thought that neutrality would be secured if they could find what each such conception *has in common*. For them this common denominator was a certain sort of experience, and I have pointed out why this will not work. But we should also be skeptical whether there is any sort of common denominator to all that can reasonably be considered good. The human good may be irreducibly various, incommensurable with respect to any single standard.

The question will thus arise whether neutrality is even possible, whether there is any possible strategy for devising a position of neutrality. I see no reason, however, to be so quickly dispirited. There is, I believe, a very familiar and understandable way of assuming a neutral posture. When two parties disagree, they can adopt a neutral stance by setting aside, for the time being, the opinions in dispute and continuing to converse on the basis of the rest of their beliefs. The sensible strategy for achieving neutrality is not to assume that the conflicting views will themselves share some common denominator (that was the classical utilitarians' conviction). Instead, the strategy is to *abstract from* what is in dispute. This is the method that I shall discuss in the next section, but I shall approach it in a somewhat indirect fashion. The best way to grasp its structure and function lies in examining why the phenomena of pluralism and reasonable disagreement in regard to ideals of the good life justify the pursuit of neutrality.

WHY NEUTRALITY?

The fact that different people hold different conceptions of the good life does not strictly entail the demand for a neutral state. Other responses are possible. The government might look to means of repression, or set up a lottery to pick the one ideal to be politically favored. Nonetheless, pluralism and disagreement about the good life do make political neutrality reasonable, and the nature of its reasonableness is what I wish to examine.

In the Preface I discussed one of the central ambiguities of the liberal tradition. Liberalism has always urged toleration for the diversity of ideals and forms of life, but almost as often it has sought to justify this position by appealing to some particular and controversial view of human flourishing. Such justifications are not improper for those who can accept their premises. It cannot be denied that these have been very influential rationales for a liberal political order. Indeed, one of liberalism's distinct strengths is the fact that there are so many different arguments appealing to different interests that converge in its favor. But a liberalism come of age cannot rest content with these arguments. Its fundamental justification must be one that forgoes any appeal to the ideals whose controversial character sets the problem, after all, for political liberalism. It must be acceptable by reasonable people having different views of the good life, not just by those who share, for example, Mill's ideal of the person.

Thus we can distinguish in general two different ways in which pluralism and disagreement with regard to the good life can be made to justify political neutrality. The first will invoke some view of human flourishing that can best be promoted if government maintains a neutral posture toward the variety of human aspirations. The most familiar arguments of this sort appeal to the values of *skepticism, experimentation*, or *individual autonomy*, respectively:

1. When ideals clash, some people conclude that there is no reason to prefer any of them, and so no government should seek to institutionalize them.

2. Other people believe that the best way to arrive at a firm conception of the good life is to participate in a number of different forms of life, comparing them and rejecting those that give us less of a sense of fulfillment. Such experimentalism would be hampered if government set out to foster only some of these ideals of the good life.

3. Others again hold that people cannot properly under-

stand what it is to have a flourishing life unless they have worked out their ideal for themselves, making their own mistakes and learning from them. Hence, no governmemt should undertake to make these decisions for people.

Each of these three arguments is well represented in the history of liberal thought and in our general culture. The skeptical argument underlies Voltaire's plea for religious toleration. The appeal to experimentalism dominates Mill's essay *On Liberty*. And the insistence upon the value of autonomy, however differently construed, unites the thought of Mill and Kant. All three make up the core of the reasons that Ackerman has recently offered for neutrality.[10]

Each of these arguments, however, will prove unacceptable to those holding different but still reasonable views about the human good – to those, that is, who do not find skepticism the proper response to deep disagreement or who do not find the values of experiment and individual autonomy so important. The fact that a conviction of mine about the meaning of life is controversial, rejected even by others whom I consider reasonable, may not offer me a sufficient reason to suspend belief in it, if it continues to make sense of my experience. An experimental spirit may be alien and destructive to some forms of life, for example, religious orthodoxies, whose claim is that in them one is to be brought up from infancy, acquiring habits and expectations that are to last a lifetime. Autonomy, too, is a value that plays a role in some conceptions of the good, but not so prominently in all; I will have more to say about this in Chapter 5.

These classical liberal arguments for neutrality will convince, therefore, only those who believe some things about the nature of human flourishing that others will not accept, and for reasons that are not without any merit. Thus when Ackerman asserts that liberal theory contains "an insistence that the forms of social life be rooted in the self-conscious value affirmations of autonomous individuals," he is invoking one of liberalism's most influential arguments for political neutrality, but he has not himself assumed a neutral position with respect to controversial ideals of the good life.[11]

Controversy about ideals of the good life and the demand that the state remain neutral toward them have been the central ingredients of the liberal vision of politics. This means that if liberals are to follow fully the spirit of liberalism, they must also devise a *neutral justification of political neutrality*. This is a second sort of justification, one which is not easily to be found in the liberal tradition, but an imperative one for liberals to work out.

In this section I shall outline how such a neutral justification would proceed, and then in subsequent sections I shall explore in more detail various aspects of the argument.

The neutral justification of political neutrality is based upon what I believe is a universal norm of rational dialogue. When two people disagree about some specific point, but wish to continue talking about the more general problem they wish to solve, each should prescind from the beliefs that the other rejects, (1) in order to construct an argument on the basis of his other beliefs that will convince the other of the truth of the disputed belief, or (2) in order to shift to another aspect of the problem, where the possibilities of agreement seem greater. In the face of disagreement, those who wish to continue the conversation should retreat to *neutral ground*, with the hope either of resolving the dispute or of bypassing it. Thus abstracting from a controversial belief does not imply that one believes it any less, that one has had reason to become skeptical toward it. One can remain as convinced of its truth as before, but for the purposes of the conversation one sets it aside. Observe also that the aim of this maneuver is not to provide an opportunity for experiments in living nor to enhance the autonomy of the participants. The goal for the sake of which neutrality forms a response to disagreement is scarcely so controversial. One wants to keep the conversation going, in order to achieve some reasoned agreement about how to solve the problem at hand.

Now it cannot be supposed that social life, and political

activity in particular, is only conversation. *Die Weltgeschichte ist kein Weltseminar.* Nor can it be assumed that all conversations aim at reasoned agreement: Often they are also occasions for self-display, or means to dominate others, or simply ways to pass the time. Nonetheless, conversation is not foreign to the political realm. The question of what principles ought to be the basis of the state's decisions is the object of debate in almost every society. Conflicting views of the good life, in the absence of any recognized constraints, will produce conflicting answers to how this question should be resolved.

The liberal will claim that the state's decisions should accordingly be justifiable on grounds neutral with respect to these conflicting views. And this neutrality of the state can itself be justified neutrally, if the norm of rational conversation already mentioned is applied to that political debate. Let us suppose that the participants in that debate accept that norm. Then each would retreat to neutral ground in order either to convince others of the truth of that disputed aspect of his own ideal of the good life, or to elaborate principles of state action upon this neutral basis itself, without resolving that dispute. To a large extent these conflicts about the nature of the good life will remain unresolved, so neutrally justifiable political principles will generally have to be found in this second, more abstract way. In either case, political principles will have to be justifiable neutrally with respect to controversial views of the good life. In this way the norm of rational conversation would serve to shape a political culture in which the public could continue to discuss disputed views about the good life with the hope of expanding the scope of agreement, but in which it would also agree that the state's decisions cannot be justified by an appeal to the intrinsic superiority of any such view that remains disputed.

Now clearly this argument is not *morally* neutral. It relies upon a commitment to converse rationally about what ought to be collectively binding political principles, and, as I shall show later, several other normative commitments are involved as well. But this is not a weakness, for the argument does not aim at complete moral neutrality. It intends to be neutral only with regard to controversial conceptions of the good life and not to all values or norms whatsoever. Although, as I shall have occasion to observe later, it is not completely neutral in this regard either, it is very nearly so, and certainly neutral enough for practical purposes. Most importantly, the argument is neutral with regard to those controversial ideals of the person (skepticism, experimentalism, autonomy) that earlier liberals often invoked, as well as to most other views of the good life. So it will be possible to reject those so-called liberal ideals of the person, and still regard neutrality as the fundamental political value.

I want now to develop the argument further, beginning with the question, What are the norms of rational conversation? The argument I have presented owes a lot to Jürgen Habermas's recent work on a conversational model of political legitimacy, and I want to clarify where I agree and disagree with what he has written.

IDEAL CONVERSATIONS

One of Habermas's aims has been to point out a commitment to ideally rational conditions of dialogue (an "ideal speech situation") that we all at least implicitly make. He insists that whenever we put forward a claim as one for whose truth we believe we have good reasons, we are anticipating an ideally rational conversation: We are assuming that the conversation in which we have advanced the claim should conform to the norms of an ideally rational conversation. That is because to believe that we have good reasons for our claim implies the belief that in an ideally rational conversation we could vindicate our claim to others, and to put forward our claim to others in the actual conversation as a claim backed up by good reasons is to assert, in effect, that these good reasons should command the assent of others.[12] With this point, put at this level of generality, I am in agreement. Whereas many conversations do not chiefly consist in putting forward claims supposedly backed up by good reasons, few conversations are altogether without this element. Habermas's argument indicates the lever by which people can be pried into accepting the commitment to rational norms of conversation that underlies the argument for political neutrality.

But there is an important respect in which I do not agree with how Habermas understands the "ideal speech situation." I must make this disagreement clear, or otherwise my appeal to norms of rational conversation will be misunderstood, and the connection of my argument to the contextualist model of justification, discussed earlier, will be obscure.

Before laying out this disagreement, I should first note that my concern is not with the nature of truth, with what it is for some claim to be true. I am not supposing that the truth of a claim consists in its being the object of agreement under ideally rational conditions. This is Habermas's consensus theory of truth, which is not implied by the argument of his that I have just recounted.[13] Such a theory of truth seems dangerously circular: What makes ideal conditions "ideal," if not their suitability for arriving at the truth? "Ideal" conditions, I believe, fix not our notion of truth, but rather our notion of justification. They provide whatever we would think the best means for arriving at the truth.

It is on the nature of justification that my disagreement with Habermas rests. He usually understands ideal conditions of justification as completely transcendent, unconditioned by what we now believe about the world and our place in it. That is why he thinks that there is only one notion of the "ideal speech situation" to which anyone should appeal. But I do not think that everyone must appeal to the same set of "ideal" conditions, when supposing that a belief or action, for which he believes he has good reasons, would be ideally justifiable to others. This is because what we consider optimal conditions for justifying a belief or action can never depart entirely from our historical circumstances. "Ideal" conditions of justification are a function of our general view of the world and what we believe are the best ways of acquiring knowledge about it.

One sign of Habermas's altogether transcendent notion of ideal conditions of justification is the meagre specification he gives to this ideal: He says only that there must be equal chances for all to choose and use speech acts. A more systematic indication is the way he generally contrasts communicative action and discourse. "Communicative action," in his terms, is any action that aims to coordinate interaction with others by coming to an understanding with them; in the form of word or deed, it embodies a factual or normative claim that the agent proposes as rationally justifiable to others under ideal conditions. When such claims meet with disagreement, the parties can resort to a "discourse" (*Diskurs*) in which they try to determine its validity by rational argument. A discourse, then, is an attempt to realize the ideal. Now Habermas has always been quite fond of underlining the differences between communicative action and discourse: In the former, background knowledge is naively presupposed, whereas in the latter, problematized claims are discussed.[14] So sharp a contrast easily implies that in discourse we carry out a radical break with our background knowledge as a whole, and this would mean that the ideal conditions we were seeking to approximate would lack any connection with our present convictions about the way the world is.

Here has arisen the great dilemma pointed out by Habermas's critics.[15] If we imagine that under ideal conditions others continue to hold their view of the world, and that view is significantly different from our own (imagine them to be the Bororo, or Tutankhamen and Li Po), we cannot expect that they could come to agree with us about the justification of some substantial claims of ours. And if, as Habermas seems to prefer, we imagine the supposedly ideal conditions as detached from our general view of the world as well as from theirs, we have no good notion of what would take place, if anything, and it is certainly unclear what sense there would be to saying that it is with the Bororo that we would be conversing. The quandary can be avoided, however, if the ideal conditions in which someone supposes his claim would be vindicated to others are understood as including what *he* considers to be the correct general view of the world and of ways of acquiring knowledge about it. Discourse, as the attempt to realize this ideal, would not therefore break with one's background knowledge, but instead would suspend judgment only about the claims under discussion. Justification would proceed *contextually*, in the way that I outlined in the previous chapter.

What, then, is exactly the nature of the agreement to which we suppose that everyone, including the Bororo, would be party when we hold that some belief or action of ours is rational? It is a conditional agreement. We are assuming that everyone, *if* he could appreciate what makes certain epistemic conditions ideal, would agree under those conditions that our claim is justified. Clearly the Bororo would not immediately share or appreciate our notion of ideal conditions, but that is no matter: In believing that our conditions are ideal, we suppose that through an indefinitely long learning process, any rational agent would come to accept them. So understood, the ideal conversation to which we appeal when we believe we have a good reason for something is neither inscrutably remote nor circular. From time to time Habermas himself, contrary to his usual manner of dealing with the ideal, has come to see things this way.[16]

Now a consequence of this way of understanding the notion of "ideal conditions of rational argument" is that when individuals' conceptions of the good life conflict, they often will also have somewhat different notions of the ideal conditions under which they believe they could justify their conception to others. This explains in part why agreement among reasonable persons is so difficult to attain in this area. But it does not imperil the neutral justification of political neutrality sketched above. That is, it does not imply that in applying his idea of the norms of rational conversation to political discussion, an individual must insist that everyone abide by beliefs that in fact will privilege his own conception of the good life. For despite these differences between individuals' notions of ideal conversation, the concept of ideally rational conditions contains some invariants. The most important one for the purposes of a neutral justification of political neutrality is the maxim already discussed: When disagreement arises, those wishing to continue the conversation should withdraw to neutral ground, in order either to resolve the dispute or, if that cannot be done rationally, to bypass it. This maxim applies even when the disagreement centers on the more substantial parts of what one understands to be ideal conditions of conversation. So one ought to prescind from these, too, if one wants to keep talking about the larger problem at hand. Since there is little chance that this disagreement will be resoluble from neutral ground, the conclusion must be that one ought to devise political principles that are themselves neutral, that do not require for their justification the ideas of the good in dispute.

EQUAL RESPECT

Their is another unavoidable question that needs to be answered about this neutral justification of political neutrality. Different individuals with different conceptions of the good life can be understood as initially placing different demands upon what ought to be collectively binding political principles. In the face of this disagreement, I have said that a common norm of rational argument requires that if the individuals still want to talk about what political principles to establish, they retreat to neutral ground. But, we may ask, why should any of them feel obliged to continue the conversation? Why should they not resort to other means (force, deceit) of establishing political principles?

In part this is not a very serious question. When those with whom we are in disagreement have views for which we nonetheless feel some sympathy, or possess along with others who share their views some significant amount of power, the reasons for continuing the conversation are obvious.

Some sense of community and a desire for civil peace will suffice in these cases to keep the conversation going. But the question does take on a real importance when we consider why we should continue to talk with those who neither stand at least close to us in their views nor have enough power to make us pay attention. Why should we continue the conversation with them? After all, continuing the conversation with those who are similar to us or who are powerful will in the end commit us to finding political principles of already considerable neutrality. Why should we be ready to increase their neutrality for the sake of those who are so unlike us and so powerless?

Let me pause to set down two conditions that an adequate answer to this question must fulfill. First, and most obviously, this justification of political neutrality can remain neutral only if the reasons for continuing the conversation with these people are neutral ones in the sense I described earlier – neutral with respect to controversial ideals of the good life. The two reasons that I have given for the less problematic cases are comparatively neutral in this sense. Sympathy is neutral to the extent of its scope, but of course its scope is limited. A desire for civil peace is compatible with a great many conceptions of the good life. For many fanatics and would-be martyrs, however, civil peace is not so important. Here, then, is a limit to the neutrality of my argument for political neutrality, but it is not, I think, a very grave one. Why must a political value be made justifiable to those who are scarcely interested in rational debate about justification anyway? A liberal political system need not feel obliged to reason with fanatics; it must simply take the necessary precautions to guard against them. Our present question is whether there exist similarly neutral reasons for continuing to talk with those who lack the power to call on our desire for civil peace and whose ideals seem quite foreign to ours. Once again, I am not denying that some conceptions of the good life would encourage further talk with them, and that such justifications are fine for those persuaded by them. But my object is a different sort of argument.

Equal respect

The second condition is that the reasons for continuing the conversation cannot be expected to follow from the notion of rationality alone. To an important extent, my neutral justification of political neutrality has relied upon what I have called a norm of rational conversation. But there are limits to what the bare idea of rationality can establish. Even if it constrains how a conversation should develop, it cannot alone justify that the conversation be undertaken. Thus, the reasons for continuing the conversation in the face of disagreement will have to embody more substantive commitments than just a commitment to reason. I have already invoked two such further commitments: sympathy with those whose ideals are similar to ours, and a desire for civil peace. These are rather substantive commitments, although they are largely neutral with respect to controversial ideals of the good life. The problem at hand is whether there is some additional commitment, of a similar neutrality, that would justify our continuing the conversation with those who are strange and weak. It must be a commitment that is morally more substantive than the bare idea of rationality, but that is not part of any disputed notion of the good life.

The answer I propose is that the neutral reason for continuing the conversation with them must lie in the wish to show everyone *equal respect*.[17] This is a term with many different senses, of course, some of them expressing rather substantive obligations toward others, so I shall clarify the rather minimalist sense in which I intend to use it.

One sense of equal respect is certainly far too weak for my purposes, and it should be set aside from the outset: This is that to treat someone with equal respect is to treat him or her as one treats others unless there is a sufficient reason not to do so. I shall mean more than this quite empty form of impartiality. Other senses are too substantive, for example, those more properly put under the heading of "egalitarianism," which require equal distribution of certain basic resources or equality of opportunity. Such substantive principles of equality may well be what neutral political principles would require in certain circumstances. But this result ought not to be incorporated into the reasons one should have for, in effect, embracing political neutrality.

The sense of equal respect to which I shall appeal lies between these two extremes, but it is not an easy concept to articulate. It is roughly that however much we may disagree with others and repudiate what they stand for, we cannot treat them merely as objects of our will, but owe them an explanation for those actions of ours that affect them. It corresponds to what Kant understood by treating another never simply as a means but also as an end, and what Dworkin calls the treatment of others as equals (as opposed to the equal treatment of them, which is a substantive egalitarian ideal).[18] In order to make this notion as intelligible as possible, I shall begin by examining what can be meant by respect.

Respect is best understood in contrast with sympathy. Both respect and sympathy constitute ways of treating others "acceptingly" even when we disagree with their beliefs. Our ability to share sympathetically another person's belief turns on our believing that in his situation we should see things that way, too. Whether we sympathize or not will depend then on our own beliefs and commitments, so we can enlarge our sympathy for others by putting a bit of distance between ourselves and those of our beliefs that would otherwise stand in the way. This is what Hume meant in saying that by "reflection" we can model our sympathy on that of a hypothetical impartial spectator.[19] A sympathetic spectator who was fully impartial would imaginatively share all beliefs whatsoever. Now since sympathy consists in an imaginative extension of our own beliefs, in an ability to imagine another's outlook as being our own, the impartial spectator can be supposed to decide between conflicting preferences by whatever principles of rational choice a single individual ought to use in ranking his own preferences. This assimilation of social choice to the model of individual choice is one of the mainstays of the utilitarian outlook: Just as an individual can be thought to have no reason not to choose his own overall welfare, however understood, over a conflicting personal preference, so there is thought to be no reason not to sacrifice an individual's preferences to the general welfare when these conflict.[20] In this way sympathy does not heed the separateness of persons. It is the notion of respect that accomplishes this.

In order to clarify the difference between sympathy and respect, let us distinguish rather crudely between a person's "situation," or the problem he must solve, and his "perspective," or the background commitments with which he confronts this problem and which lead to his forming some preference or belief to deal with the problem. Then if we disagree with his preference or belief, but still wish to treat him acceptingly, we have two alternatives before us. Sympathizing with another's belief consists in believing that in his situation it would have been our own, so we can broaden our sympathy to the extent we can imagine sharing another's perspective. On the other hand, respecting another belief implies recognizing that from his perspective it was justifiably his, whether or not we can imagine sharing his perspective, and so his belief in that situation. Whereas sympathy involves an imaginative extension of our own person, our beliefs and perspective, respect heeds the distinctness of persons. The extent to which we either respect or sympathize with another's belief will depend upon how much of his perspective we are willing to imagine ourselves sharing. The more we thus identify ourselves with him, the more our respect will become sympathy. Nonetheless, the important point is that to the extent that we hold on to our own perspective, we can respect his views without sympathizing with them. We can find them justified from his perspective, without believing that they would be ours in that situation.

Respect, as discussed so far, has been respect for some *belief* held by another. But the sort of respect with which I am concerned is a respect for *persons*. This amplified notion of respect for persons grows out of the more restrictive one, I believe, when we recognize other persons as being capable of coherently developing beliefs from within their own perspective (although not necessarily on their own, or autonomously), whether or not their actual beliefs are indeed justified from their point of view. To have respect for a person is to view him as capable of elaborating beliefs that we would respect.[21]

Now there are two significant differences between respect for beliefs and respect for persons. Respect for beliefs is simply a belief about their justifiability within the other's perspective; so it is not itself an obligation we could bear toward others. Respect for persons, however, is not just a belief that others have a capacity for developing beliefs justifiable within their own perspective, and it cannot be simply deduced (even by "analysis of concepts") from that fact; it is an obligation to treat others in a certain way because of that fact (in what way, I shall come to shortly). Furthermore, respect for beliefs is not something that anyone can be expected to accord equally to all. Some beliefs deserve it, others do not. By contrast, a capacity for working out a coherent view of the world is one that everyone (except some of the clinically insane) possesses. So respect for persons, as an attitude involving recognition of this capacity, is something that we can show equally to others. Of course, some people have this capacity to a greater degree than others do, but respect is something that others as persons are due just by virtue of having that capacity, so it should be given equally to all.[22]

What is precisely then the obligation of equal respect that we should show others in virtue of their having the capacity to work out their own view of the world? Whatever we do that affects another is something with which he must deal from within his own perspective. When he demands that we justify our action to him, he is recognizing that we, too, have a perspective on the world in which presumably our action makes sense, and indicating his willingness to discuss it rationally with us (of course, his notion of rational discussion may differ substantially from ours, as I noted earlier). The *obligation* of equal respect consists in our being obligated to treat another as he is treating us – to use his having a perspective on the world as a reason for discussing the merits of our action rationally with him (in the light of how we understand a rational discussion). This is the way in which equal respect involves mutual respect, as Hegel understood.

I have discussed respect at such length for two reasons. First, previous treatments of respect have usually been rather vague, passing over the difference and connection between the two sorts of respect, as well as the rationale for the obligation of equal respect. Just as importantly, we can now see why the obligation of equal respect will lead one to continue the conversation about political principles even with those who lack other means (similarity or power) of interesting one in this. To show another equal respect is to treat his demand for justification as part of a rational discussion one must have with him. Even if two people disagree significantly about what would be the ideal conditions under which this discussion should proceed, they will both agree that this disagreement is reason to retreat to neutral ground and proceed from there.

Does equal respect, so understood, satisfy the two conditions I laid down at the beginning? It is certainly not an obligation we should accept just by virtue of being rational beings, for there is nothing contrary to reason in refusing to treat others as they treat us. So the second condition is satisfied. What about the first? Is equal respect a *neutral* reason, in the sense of being impartial between conflicting views of the good life? I believe that it is largely neutral. Respect for persons is an attitude that we can adopt, just about however much we may disagree with them about the nature of the good life. It certainly seems clear that when equal respect requires us to treat acceptingly those who disagree with us, it is not for the obviously nonneutral reasons that classical liberals have often given for adopting the stance of political neutrality. Others are due equal respect by virtue of their capacity for working out a coherent view of the world and indeed of the good life, whether or not they exercise this capacity autonomously and experimentally, or through the uncritical acceptance of traditions and forms of life. Equal respect does not demand that we approve of people working out their ideals autonomously or in an experimentalist spirit.

We could repudiate the value of autonomy or experimentalism and take steps to discourage it in others, while still consistently feeling obliged to explain the merits of these actions to those who took exception to them.

I do not mean to suggest that a commitment to equal respect has been a perennial feature of human culture. Clearly it has not been such, and there are surely specific historical conditions that make this commitment relatively widespread today. I wish to insist only that it is *compatible* with a very great variety of ideals of the good life, including those that were dominant at times when, as a matter of fact, the norm of equal respect was not so widely shared. For example, the belief that some particular hereditary class produces those most fit to rule does not exclude equal respect, for one could feel obliged (as some such aristocrats were) to justify this belief to the other classes.

However, some views of the good life – some especially virulent forms of racism, for example – must reject the obligation of equal respect in order to remain consistent. But once again I do not believe that this forms a significant limit to the neutrality of my argument. Liberals need not have an argument to convince people of this sort, only safeguards for preventing them from acquiring political power. After all, such people seem little interested in rational argument.

Let me close, nonetheless, on a more modest note. Whatever the limits to its neutrality, equal respect is neutral with respect to the ideals of skepticism, experimentalism, and autonomy. Consequently, the justification of political neutrality that I have developed is more neutral than the classical justification that appealed to those ideals, and so – most importantly – it can work for those who do not share those ideals. As I shall show in the next chapters, the controversial character of these ideals has been a central reason for opposition to liberalism. My neutral justification of liberalism seems the best way for liberals to meet this form of criticism.

PRACTICAL LIMITS

This completes the neutral justification of political neutral-ality. A commitment to treating others with equal respect forms the ultimate reason why in the face of disagreement we should keep the conversation going, and to do that, of course, we must retreat to neutral ground.

There remains, however, one final objection to this argu-ment for the distinctive feature of a liberal political order. Even if this argument is faultless, some will complain, the obvious fact is that "neutral ground" offers too weak a basis for deriving any political principles that assign basic liberties and distribute wealth. Neutrality is powerless, the objection claims, as a method for solving the fundamental problem of politics. As a result, actual political systems that call them-selves liberal must be either confused or disingenuous.

This objection is serious, but it should not ultimately dis-comfit the liberal. We should first observe that political neu-trality, as I have described it, is a relative matter. It does not require that the state be neutral with respect to all concep-tions of the good life, but only with respect to those actually disputed in the society. Where everyone agrees about some element of human flourishing, the liberal should have no reason to deny it a role in shaping political principles.

Nonetheless, the objection could be reformulated to say that in any society such as ours where disagreement about the good life extends so deeply, even a relative neutrality will lack the content necessary for elaborating political prin-ciples. The most direct way to deal with this objection, of course, would be to examine how far this is true of particular societies. But I believe that the proper response should re-main at a higher level of generality. There is no reason, I think, why a liberal should have to dispute the fact that full neutrality in a modern society may prove too empty to gen-erate any substantive political principles. Neutrality, how-ever, is not the liberal's only desideratum. There is also the need for some decision to be made about what should be the principles governing basic liberties and distribution. So the liberal must be willing to consider tradeoffs between these two goals. If full neutrality makes such a decision impossible, then neutrality should be made more restrictive until a decision does become possible.

The important point for the liberal is that such tradeoffs can still be devised in the spirit of neutrality. Guiding them will be a principle embodying a higher neutrality; namely, that one should institute only the least abridgment of neutrality necessary for making a decision possible. Thus, if a certain view about the good life with which some people disagree is nonetheless admitted by the liberal as part of the basis for deciding about substantive political principles, this will not be because he assumes it to be true. Instead, this will be because he believes that admitting it will constitute the least restriction of neutrality necessary for arriving at an adequate basis for the decisions needing to be made.

In what, however, does the "least restriction" consist? There appear to be two different dimensions along which a minimum, in the spirit of neutrality, could be sought:

1. One could admit beliefs that are the least central to anyone's idea of the good life, or
2. One could admit beliefs that the least number of people do not hold.

The first dimension is the more neutral alternative, but in many cases it may prove impossible to implement, and then one must resort to the second.

Political neutrality, therefore, can be both a justifiable and a practicable ideal. My chief concern in this chapter has been to show how this ideal can be justified neutrally, without need for appeal to any disputed notion of the good life. I must insist once again that I do not hold a neutral justification to be the only justification for neutrality. But I do consider it the only mode of justification fully within the liberal spirit. For the fact that lies at the heart of liberalism is that reasonable people differ and disagree about the nature of the good life.

Chapter 4

The political order and personal ideals

For modern liberal societies the primary value of the political order must be the neutrality of the state. The fundamental political principles by which all are to live must be justifiable without appeal to the intrinsic superiority of any controversial ideal of the good life. Now such principles will assign to persons rights and duties having to do with how the advantages of social cooperation are to be distributed among them. They are therefore principles of justice. By virtue of their neutrality, liberal principles of justice embody one instance of Kant's claim that the right must be prior to the good.[1] Principles of justice must be justifiable antecedently to disputed notions of the good life. For two reasons, however, this similarity to Kantianism should not be pressed too far. Political neutrality need not be absolute, as Kant intended his principle to be: It need extend only to controversial ideals of the good life, and not to those that are shared. Just as importantly, the priority of the right over the good, as I have so far explained it, is a *political* ideal. Nothing has been said to imply that this priority must extend to the whole of morality, as Kant believed it did. In particular, nothing I have said should imply that in our *personal* ideals, in our ideals of what we should be as persons outside the political realm, we must have a greater allegiance to neutrality than to our own conception of the good life.

In this chapter I want to explore further the problem of what liberalism has to say about the relation between political and personal ideals. I shall be concerned to defend a certain form of myopia: What is of paramount importance in the political realm need not have the same weight outside that realm. Neutrality can be our highest political value, without being the value we must strive to make supreme in other parts of our lives, without being, as I shall use this term, our highest "personal ideal."

This problem is so important, not only because it points to some of the complexity that liberalism must embody, but also because it is the crux on which many of the most important criticisms of liberalism have turned. For reasons that I shall examine, Kant believed that our highest personal ideal ought to incorporate a certain distance or detachment toward conceptions of the good life that take in more than just the dictates of universal morality. This personal ideal has the same priorities as the liberal political ideal of neutrality and, Kant believed, would serve to justify it. Tying the defense of liberalism to so controversial an ideal of the person was a very shaky tactic. As I argued in the previous chapter, liberalism has been a response to the lack of consensus about notions of the good life, and ideals of the person are inseparable from these. In addition, this Kantian approach has made it easier for antiliberals – from German Romanticism to the present – to appear more solid about political matters, simply because they have raised serious doubts about the Kantian ideal of the person. I shall discuss such antiliberal criticisms more thoroughly in the next chapter. Here I want to look somewhat systematically at the relation between the political ideal of neutrality and our attachment to various views of the good life, and then to examine Kant's reasons for understanding that relation as he did.

LIBERAL JUSTICE AS A MODUS VIVENDI

Hume wrote that justice is an "artificial" virtue. Not all of what he said specifically about what makes a virtue "artificial" seems to me acceptable. In particular, what distinguishes an artificial virtue from a natural one (such as courage) cannot be that it fails to be "instinctive," as Hume wrote, for surely the cultivation and articulation of courage and benevolence, no less than justice, depend upon training and social circumstance. But despite his reliance on this dubious eighteenth-century notion of nature, Hume's idea that justice is an artificial virtue contains an important truth. The artificiality of justice also meant for him that it is a device or convention that human beings set up to solve a certain problem that has arisen because of their other values and commitments.[2] By contrast, virtues such as courage or benevolence do not have this basically second-order character; the aim of a benevolent action is primarily to help the person in need, and not to adjudicate other values. The importance of this point is that it lets us see how a commitment to justice, and to the liberal ideal of neutrality, within the political realm can coexist with commitments to particular visions of the good life outside it.

Let us look at what Hume thought was the problem to which the convention of justice is the solution – namely, the "circumstances of justice."[3] These circumstances fall into two groups. The *external circumstances* include the relative scarcity of most of the things that human beings need and want and the relative instability of their possession (the things we possess do not become inseparable extensions of our body but can be taken from us). The *internal circumstances* consist in the different ultimate purposes that human beings pursue, and so in the conflicting claims that people make upon what political principles should regulate the benefits of social cooperation. Hume considered that these purposes conflict because our conceptions of the good life are either egoistic or particularistic enough that our generosity would extend chiefly to our family, friends, and associates, and not to society as a whole. This characterization of human nature may strike some as an ideological parti pris. Capitalism, it is often said, has shackled our fellow-feeling. Now, nostalgia about precapitalist societies and their supposedly "organic bonds of solidarity" is surely fantastical. Nonetheless, let us suppose that the future might harbor possibilities of social con-

71

duct so far unknown to history, or to "human prehistory", as Marxists say. Let us suppose that human beings developed a strong habit of universal benevolence, their conception of the good life being one that required that an impartial concern for all weigh more than particularistic concerns for a specific few. (And let us put aside the question whether this would be for the best.) Even then, the circumstance of deeply conflicting claims upon the choice of political principles would doubtlessly remain. A situation where everyone is motivated by a paramount concern for everyone else need not be one where everyone agrees about the content of the good life. However benevolently inclined, A may not agree with B about what is in B's interest; and even if A and B both wish to promote the public interest, they may not share a common conception of what that is. A genuine concern for the welfare of others harbors no guarantee of consensus. Indeed, disagreement is what we should expect when people have the time to work out their views about the good life. So unless we conjoin with the utopian hypothesis of universal benevolence the equally improbable hypotheses of unanimity of opinion and coincidence of interests, the internal circumstances of justice – the conflict between conceptions of the good life – will remain.

These are considerations with which Kant supplemented Hume's account of the internal circumstances of justice.[4] They underlie his insistence that the idea of happiness cannot serve as the moral basis of a political order. Kant's point here should not be viewed simply as an incipient critique of utilitarianism, although that, too, was surely involved from his reading of Hutcheson. (Nor is it necessarily tied to his idea of the nonempirical basis of morality, which I shall discuss later.) More importantly, contained in it was the conviction that conceptions of happiness are something that different individuals are bound to develop and articulate differently. "Man kann nicht glücklich sein, ohne nach seinem Begriff von Glückseligkeit."[5] Since conceptions of happiness are bound to diverge, Kant reasoned, the common principles by which human beings must agree to live together should not implement any one of these conceptions.[6] Moreover, the diversity of happiness that Kant in his systematic works generally described as a given condition, he recognized in his writings on the philosophy of history as something subject to historical development (see "Ideen zu einer allgemeinen Geschichte in weltbürgerlicher Absicht."). Thus, the internal circumstances of justice comprise those two characteristically modern phenomena – the pluralism of ideals of the good life and the existence of reasonable disagreement about which ideals are preferable – that stand at the center of liberal political thought. Neutral principles of justice are the solution that liberals (such as Hume and, even more so, Kant) have urged for the political problems that these competing ideals produce.

It is the relation between the internal circumstances of justice and neutral principles of justice that I want to examine. Political neutrality requires that the conflicting ideals of the good life be set aside in the political realm; that is, the fundamental political principles should be ones whose justification does not depend on assuming the intrinsic superiority of any of these contested ideals. In other words, what is of the highest importance in the circumstances of justice, our own conception of the ends of life, will not function as the paramount value of a liberal political order. The crucial question is how we should understand this difference in priorities.

There are two distinct sorts of answers to this question, which I shall designate the *modus vivendi* and the *expressivist* perspectives. Before explaining the difference between these two, I want first to introduce another distinction, one between what I shall call "substantial" ideals of the good life and the ideals of autonomy and experimentalism that I discussed earlier. Substantial ideals involve commitment to some specific way of life. They may be narrow or broad in the interests that they seek to advance, but in any case they embody a specific structure of purposes, significances, and activities: There is the life devoted to art, or the missionary life, or the life centered on family or job. By contrast, the ideals of autonomy and experimentalism concern the way in which we ought to assume and pursue such substantial ideals. They themselves are not so much ways of life as attitudes in which we are to understand our commitment to ways of life. Autonomy is an ideal that demands that we undertake a specific way of life, making its purposes and significances our own, only in the light of critically evaluating on our own its strengths and weaknesses, comparing them with those of other available ways of life. The closely related ideal of experimentalism urges that ways of life are to be treated much as scientific theories, our attachment to them never so close that we could not give them up with equanimity in the face of recalcitrant experience. The distinction between these two sorts of personal ideals will prove indispensable in analyzing the modus vivendi and expressivist views of political neutrality.

Now the modus vivendi view is the one most readily suggested by the argument for political neutrality that I developed in the preceding chapter. In order to take up a neutral position by abstracting from our substantial conception of the good life, we are not, I said, repudiating that conception or lessening our attachment to it. We have not adopted a general posture of neutrality or detachment toward our idea of what makes life worth living. That idea may remain so close to us, so "constitutive" (as I shall say) of what we understand to be of ultimate significance, that we would be unwilling to accept in imagination our lives without it. But we are declining to appeal to it for a particular purpose – that of devising common political principles. Neutrality is simply a means of accommodation. It is a stance that we adopt in order to solve a specific problem to which our various commitments give rise, and so it is not a stance that expresses our full understanding of our purposes. It establishes a modus vivendi between persons whose ultimate ideals do not coincide.

A number of different considerations move us to take up such a stance. There is, first of all, a norm of rational conversation, I have argued, that requires that if we want to solve some problem but encounter disagreement about how to do so, we should retreat to neutral ground. Then, there are the reasons we have for wanting to converse with others about what political principles to adopt. Besides a desire for civil peace and sympathy for those whose ideals are similar to ours, the norm of equal respect demands that we explain our proposals to those whom they will affect. To these reasons may be added the likelihood that our pursuit of some substantial ideal of the good life will be protected if others, with different ideals, also agree that common political principles must be sought from neutral ground. The important fact about all these reasons is that none of them calls for any weakening of our allegiance to what we understand as the fulfilled life. Only the norm of equal respect might seem to belie this point, but remember how comparatively weak this norm is. It does not imply that every conception of the good life merits equivalent respect; if it did so, of course, it would undermine in many cases the special hold that our own ultimate purposes have upon us. However, the norm of equal respect is directed not toward ideals, but rather toward persons. It requires that no one can be a mere object of our will, that each is due an explanation of why we pursue some ideal of the good life, if that pursuit affects his own projects.

The modus vivendi view of political neutrality thus allows our substantial notion of the good to remain paramount outside the political realm. The priority of the right over the good, the demand for neutrality toward conflicting ideas of the good, serves only as a political principle, governing the relations among people as *citizens*. In the political realm neutrality must be supreme, and our substantial ideas of the good life, if controversial, must give way before it. But it need not extend further, and it will not do so, where people have constitutive attachments to some such substantial vision. Neutrality will rarely figure as the cardinal virtue of intermediate associations such as church, family, or ethnic group.

This divergence between *citoyen* and *homme*, between the "public" (the political) and the "private" (the nonpolitical), lies at the heart of the modus vivendi view. Liberalism is seen thus as an "art of separation," opposed to the idea of society as an organic whole.[7] This view finds its paradigmatic exposition in the toleration theories of Bodin, Locke, and Bayle, for whom the supreme importance of religion is compatible with the fact that the state should aim at civil peace rather than salvation.[8] And it has been the object of opprobrium for those political thinkers from Rousseau to Marx and beyond who, seeing this differentiation of realms as the rift of "alienation," have sought to defend the "wholeness" of man. About this form of antiliberalism I shall have more to say in the next chapter.

The modus vivendi perspective is not the only one that we could have toward the relation between political neutrality and substantial conceptions of the good life. Instead of regarding the neutrality of the state as a means of accommodation, we could adopt the expressivist perspective toward political neutrality that was Kant's. That is, we could understand political neutrality as expressing the very sort of detachment we ought to have in general toward any substantial ideal of human flourishing. To the neutrality of the state would correspond the autonomy of the individual as our highest personal ideal, for the autonomous person sustains a certain distance toward his substantial ideal of the good. Because this substantial ideal is his only because he has freely made it his, it cannot be constitutive of his understanding of what is of paramount importance to him. His highest ideal remains his autonomy, not the substantial ideal he autonomously chooses.

This expressivist perspective toward political neutrality is one instance of a more general position. Political expressivism, in general, demands that our highest political ideal be mirrored in our highest personal ideal, that is, in our ideal of what should have paramount importance in the rest of our lives. Political expressivism need not embody a commitment to liberalism, and indeed it has been most frequently connected with the nonliberal view that the state must foster some substantial ideal of the good life in its citizens or subjects. Nonetheless, in its liberal form it encompasses Kant's understanding of the relation between political and personal ideals. In both, he insisted, the right must be prior to the good, so that in our personal ideal we must sustain the same sort of distance toward substantial ideals of the good as does the neutral state. This will be so, if our highest personal ideal is autonomy.

I doubt whether this expressivist version of liberalism can be successfully defended. I am convinced that it is not a doctrine that must be adopted if liberalism is to be viable. This is because there remains the modus vivendi version that I have examined in the preceding chapter and in this. A commitment to political neutrality, the acceptance of justice as a device of accommodation between persons having different personal ideals, does not require allegiance to any ideal so controversial as that of autonomy. In the next section I shall show why, contrary to Kant, we do not *have to* make the right prior to the good in our personal ideal. This line of thought will also suggest that we *should not* make autonomy paramount, and in the following chapter I shall develop this point further in examining the antiliberal positions of some of Kant's successors. Their insistence upon the value of tradition and the social character of the self can be preserved apart from their antiliberalism, so long as we understand political neutrality as a modus vivendi.

KANTIAN LIBERALISM

Kant did not believe that we should understand the neutrality of justice simply as the modus vivendi that I have described in the preceding pages. Abstracting from our own conception of the good life is not, for him, something we do for the particular purpose of arriving at common political principles. Instead, Kant held that maintaining a certain distance toward such conceptions should shape our lives throughout, because it is an emblem of our nature as moral beings. Our moral nature is what requires us never to identify ourselves so closely with any vision of the good life that it becomes "constitutive" of our self-understanding; we must never let ourselves grow so attached to such a vision that we are unwilling to imagine ourselves without it. Indeed, Kant thought that this sort of detachment should be a central premise in justifying the neutrality of the state.

Central to Kant's position here is the ideal of autonomy. In his essay "Was ist Aufklärung?" Kant laid out some of what this ideal involves. *Sapere aude*, he wrote: learn to evaluate social institutions and practices on your own, resist the "self-imposed immaturity" of trusting in the authority of others. This ideal urges a critical self-transparency that may be impossible to achieve fully; in so unqualified a form, it may also be an ideal whose full implementation we ought not to desire. But before dealing with these difficult questions, we must look more carefully at the nature of this ideal and at the reasons that Kant had for espousing it.

Kant came to see that one of the distinctive features of his moral theory was a general priority of the right over the good. He did not, in fact, come to see it on his own, for Pistorius first pointed it out in his review of the *Grundlegung zur Metaphysik der Sitten* (1785); but Kant put it at the center of his exposition in the *Kritik der praktischen Vernunft* (1788). The meaning of that priority is this. To place the concept of the good at the foundations of morality would be to make what we ought to do a function of what as a matter of fact we would desire, had we the appropriate knowledge of our happiness or our perfection. In company with a long tradition stretching back to the Greeks, Kant took the good to be an attractive and not an imperative notion. Whatever we hold to be good is something that we do desire, and to say that one ought to desire X because it is good amounts to predicting that if one knew enough about X, one would indeed desire it. In addition, Kant drew from this tradition the idea that good is an empirical notion, in the sense that what we hold to be good depends upon our experience. There is no a priori concept of happiness and perfection, so the good is always the object of an empirically conditioned desire. The fact is, Kant insisted, that experience does not yield any shared and sufficiently determinate idea of happiness and perfection. Consequently, the notion of good cannot lie at the basis of morality. Instead, the imperative notion of the right, the idea that we ought to perform certain actions, must be funda- mental. Making the right prior to the good means that our obligation to do A cannot be based in our having or (with appropriate knowledge) coming to have an empirically con- ditioned desire to do A. The moral law is pure of empirical contingencies. It is "categorical."[9]

One very important consequence of this maneuver is that Kant's notion of morality is inherently universalistic. Moral obligations apply to everyone, Kant held, whatever his em- pirically conditioned desires. Whereas I do not have to repay a debt unless it is an empirical fact that I have borrowed, this duty is not mine because I have an empirically conditioned desire to observe it; anyone who has borrowed ought to repay, whether he wants to or not. However, we should not simply take it for granted that the whole of morality is uni- versalistic. Contrast, for example, the duty of repaying debts with the duties of friendship. I have no obligation to treat someone in accord with what friendship demands, unless I have, as a matter of empirical fact, the desire to be friends with that person. It would be a desiccated idea of friendship, indeed a travesty of it, to say that I should treat some person as a friend, whether I want to or not. So the priority of the right over the good excludes from the domain of morality particularistic duties such as those of friendship and of art and those that often arise from our membership in specific social institutions. As a matter of mere classification, this is innocuous. But Kant's priority of the right over the good also meant that universalistic morality should always take prec- edence over "my station and its duties," as Bradley put it; and this is far from unquestionable.[10]

The conflict between universalistic and particularistic du- ties is a phenomenon about which I shall have something to say in the last chapter of this book. Here I want to track the thought that moved Kant to make universalistic morality our paramount obligation.

Particularistic duties are, by their very nature, empirically conditioned; they involve, as Kant would say, "hypothetical," not "categorical" imperatives. So, too, are substantial conceptions of the good life; indeed, duties of that sort grow out of the specific ways of life that such substantial ideals recommend. Consequently, it is the very same reason that urges that we maintain a certain distance toward substantial ideals of the good life that also demands that universalistic morality always be supreme. This is Kant's personal ideal of autonomy. We must now turn to his reasons for holding to this ideal.

So far I have been discussing the *scope* of moral obligations, that is, the conditions under which we can be said to have an obligation. Distinct from this is the matter of what is the *motivational basis* of moral obligations, the nature of the reasons we can have for trying to carry out what are our obligations. Kant's commitment to the ideal of autonomy stems from his understanding of the relation between these two aspects of morality.

From his belief that all moral obligations are categorical Kant inferred that any being on whom such obligations are binding must be free in a radical way. Any such being must have an empirically unconditioned interest in carrying out his obligations (although, of course, he can decide not to act on this motive). In other words, we cannot attribute to someone an obligation that is his independently of his empirically conditioned interests, unless we suppose that he has an empirically unconditioned interest in performing it.[11] This interest must indeed be a strictly moral interest (to do one's duty for its own sake), for any ulterior end would be empirically conditioned. (*Why* Kant maintained this tight fit between scope and motivational basis is a point to which I shall return.) This idea of a nonempirical freedom leads us into the heart of Kant's moral doctrine. Kant did not believe, of course, that we could ever know that we were free in this way. Our knowledge is limited to possible objects of experience, and so it cannot encompass any interest we might have apart from the nature of our experience – our personal and social circumstances, our training and socialization. But insofar as we believe ourselves to be moral beings, persons with moral obligations, we must believe, Kant held, that we are free: "Though freedom is certainly the *ratio essendi* of the moral law, the latter is the *ratio cognoscendi* of freedom."[12] It is this empirically unconditioned interest that supports the ideal of autonomy: We are to live in accord with this interest that separates us from all our other empirically conditioned interests. This interest Kant called an interest of reason *(Vernunftinteresse)*, since any rational being as such, whatever his history of experience, has sufficient motive to do what he morally ought to do. Our nonempirical freedom explains how reason alone is not inert, but practical.[13]

Aristotle denied, of course, that reason alone could ever move us to act, and this is an important sign of what ultimately separates these two moral thinkers. Aristotle believed that our interest in morality depends on our character, our habits and feelings, and that our character depends essentially upon our moral training and social circumstance. This Kant naturally denied. Moral character does not determine our acting out of a sense of duty; rather it is our freedom, unconditioned by any empirical antecedents, that creates our moral character.[14] Our true personality lies apart from empirical circumstance, and the "inclinations" that it shapes are "always burdensome to a rational being, and, though he cannot put them aside, they nevertheless elicit from him the wish to be free of them."[15] Our personal ideal, according to Kant, must thus be to identify ourselves with this transcendental personhood. Being empirically unconditioned, this freedom is ours, of course, no matter what we do. What Kant's ideal of the person asks of us is that we live in accord with it; that is, that we exercise it in ways that do not deny it, that we do not indulge in the self-imposed immaturity of trusting in the authority of others. We must seek to remain above natural and social contingencies.

These views about freedom and true personhood raise a number of difficult questions of coherence and articulation, and Kant gave more attention to these than to the simple affirmation of his ideal of the person. Chief among these difficulties were how it is that such free persons can indeed act in the empirical world and how it is that they can choose evil as well as good. They led Kant to give some further structure to his idea of freedom, most notably a distinction between the negative freedom of spontaneity or mere empirical unconditionedness *(Willkür)* and the positive freedom of autonomy in the strict sense of imposing the moral law upon oneself *(Wille)*.[16]

But these complications do not alter the basic feature of Kant's ideal of the person. Our true personality requires that, recognizing how our freedom transcends our empirically conditioned interests, we always maintain an appropriate distance toward them. We should always regard our character as freely created, and so not as a constitutive part of ourselves, not as a horizon of habits and expectations we are unwilling to imagine ourselves without. In his early Kantian period, Fichte had a good sense of the core of this ideal, even if he had not the intellectual strength to appreciate its complexities. In 1793 he wrote:

> If our true ultimate end is given to us through and in the form of our pure self through the moral law in us, then everything in us which does not belong to this pure form or which makes us sensible beings is not an end, but merely a means for our higher spiritual end.... No one *becomes* cultivated, rather everyone has to cultivate *himself*. All merely passive behavior is the exact opposite of culture; education occurs through self-activity.[17]

This is the Kantian ideal of the person. Kant conceded that our summum bonum cannot be our freedom itself, but must include some substantial ideal of the good life, some empirically conditioned notion of happiness, so long as that is in accord with morality. But within this summum bonum there remains the distinction between the true self and its contingent projects.[18]

It is on the basis of this ideal of the person that Kant preferred to argue for political neutrality. Setting aside controversial ideas of the good life (or of "happiness") in order to arrive at common political principles is not, as Kant understood it, merely a way of handling a specific problem that arises in one area of social life. Instead, it expresses the very structure of what ought to be our personal ideal. No substantial conception of happiness should be made the basis of the political order, Kant argued, because we are *free*, because we have a will that is unconditioned by empirical ends.[19] Kant did hold that political neutrality could be defended without an appeal to this notion of nonempirical freedom; thus, in his essay on *Perpetual Peace* he imagined that a society of devils could sustain a neutral state. But this is not how he thought that political neutrality ought to be understood. What should be our personal ideal urges otherwise. Political neutrality should be seen as reflecting the essential difference that we should respect between our transcendental freedom and empirically conditioned conceptions of the good life. It is not surprising, therefore, that Kant chose the political image of "a kingdom of ends" (*Reich der Zwecke*) to represent what should be our highest personal ideal. This image corresponds to his ideal of a political commonwealth: Just as in the ideal polity there is a restriction of each individual's freedom compatible with a similar restriction of the freedom of everyone else, established independently of any empirical ends of happiness, so in the kingdom of ends "we abstract from the personal differences between rational beings, and also from all the content of their private ends – to conceive a whole of all ends in systematic conjunction."[20] Kant believed, therefore, that the personal ideal of autonomy should form an indispensable part of political liberalism.

We must now turn to the important question of whether Kant is right that morality is necessarily bound up with this notion of an empirically unconditioned freedom. Only so can we determine how compelling is his version of liberalism. I indicated that he arrived at this notion of freedom by virtue of holding the following beliefs:

1. The scope of moral obligations is categorical, binding upon us whatever our empirically conditioned interests or desires.

2. The empirically unconditioned scope of morality implies that we must have an empirically unconditioned motivational basis for heeding its demands.

I believe that (1) is unobjectionable, at least in a qualified form: Not all, but certainly some, of our obligations do have a universalistic or categorical character. (Whether a categorical imperative must also be an overriding one is a problem that I shall examine in Chapter 6.) The questionable part of Kant's argument lies rather in (2). Why must we suppose that if a duty is universalistic, binding on all whatever their empirically conditioned interests, everyone must have an empirically unconditioned motive to fulfill it? Why must there be this correspondence between scope and motivational basis?

We must reject at the outset one answer that Kant gave to this question. Very often, he construed all our empirically conditioned interests, or notions of happiness, as forms of self-love – a particularly bad bit of psychology to rest so noble a doctrine of freedom upon.[21] But Kant had a better reason than just an appeal to our capacity for looking beyond our own advantage. Underlying premise (2) above was a particularly strong version of the principle that "ought" implies "can." To say that someone ought to do some action, Kant thought, makes sense only if we suppose that he now has it in his power to do it, in the sense that he now has a motive sufficient to do it (whether or not he lets the motive indeed move him to do it). An empirically unconditioned obligation thus requires there to be an empirically unconditioned motive. This assumption often lurks implicitly behind Kant's statements that categoricity of duty involves nonempirical freedom, but often he also explicitly acknowledges the central role it plays.[22]

Whether liberalism should take a Kantian form thus depends on whether we must accept this principle about "ought" and "can."

MORALITY AND MORAL PSYCHOLOGY

Before exploring this matter further I must point out that, in general, there has been not one, but two distinct matters to which the principle " 'ought' implies 'can' " has been applied. The first concerns the relation between obligation and motivation, which is the one now under discussion. The second is the different relation between obligation and feasibility: In this case " 'ought' implies 'can'" means that someone can have an obligation to do something in a particular situation only if, apart from what his motivational state may be, the action demanded is possible or performable in that situation. I have strong doubts about whether " 'ought' implies 'can'" is valid in either of these domains, and in Chapter 6 I shall look carefully at the relation between obligation and feasibility. Here it is the different relation between obligation and motivation that I want to examine. I shall be considering only universalistic obligations.

Kant supposed this relation to hold in a very strong form. For someone to have an obligation now, he must also have now a motive sufficient to move him to carry it out. This is not, however, the only way we can understand there to be a connection between obligation and motivation. We could dispense with the idea of nonempirical freedom and hold instead that someone has a (categorical) obligation only if at least one of the following conditions is satisfied:

1. He now has an empirically conditioned motive (whether expressing an *intrinsic* interest in morality or not) sufficient to do it;
2. He now could be trained or brought round to have such a motive;
3. He once had such a motive or once could have been

trained to have it, although since then he has led the sort of
life through which that capacity has withered away.

Here we have a weaker link between obligation and motivation, but one that serves to emphasize two aspects of moral
life that Kant's theory neglects. This view allows us to see
that training and socialization play an indispensable role in
our wanting to do what we ought to do, and particularly in
our wanting to do so because of its moral rightness (which
for Kant was precisely the sort of motive that is empirically
unconditioned). This view also indicates that the moral capacities that are cultivated by proper training can be diminished and even destroyed by the wrong sort of life and so
by unfavorable social circumstance. It can be, and indeed it
should be, combined with the belief that except for the men-
tally incapacitated, each of us when young has the capacity
for developing an interest in morality, a capacity that may
be realized, but also lost.

Everything seems to count in favor of this view. Unlike
Kant's, it explains the importance of training and mode of
life for our moral character, for what is our interest in morality, and for whether that interest is intrinsic or not. Thus,
by recognizing the empirically conditioned nature of this interest, this view carries none of Kant's metaphysical commitments. At the same time, we can preserve his genuine
insight that (at least some) obligations are categorical in
scope, so long as we believe that everyone has naturally the
capacity for developing an interest in morality.

This is a view that resembles Aristotle's understanding of
moral motivation, and indeed the difference between it and
Kant's view lies at the very basis of what separates Aristotelian and Kantian ethics. Aristotle did believe that moral
praise and blame can be directed only toward actions that
are voluntary, and this might seem to imply that an action
can constitute a failure of obligation only if the agent then
had it in his power to want to do what is right. But Aristotle
did not accept this implication. For him an action counts as
"voluntary" simply if its source lies in the agent, so that

86

voluntarily doing what is wrong implies not that the agent had a motive to do what is right, but only that his doing wrong comes from his character, and not from some external force (such as someone taking him by the hand to slap someone else).[23] This is confirmed by the fact that throughout Aristotle insisted upon the necessity of training to build and foster motives and that he recognized the legitimacy of blaming the wrongful actions of those whose way of life has left them without any motivational interest in morality.[24]

Once we recognize the empirical constitution of any interest that we may have in morality, we must also see that the moral worth of persons cannot be altogether disconnected from natural advantage. Some people are more easily trained than others and show a greater natural ability for appreciating moral distinctions. This can be so, even if it is also the case that everyone has a capacity for developing a motivational interest in morality. (Thus, nothing binds us to accepting Aristotle's view that a significantly large number of people, whom he called "natural slaves," are constitutionally incapable of developing such an interest.) The view of obligation and motivation that I have proposed also ties moral worth inextricably to social and historical circumstance. In all these regards, therefore, moral worth cannot transcend moral luck. The sort of interest that we acquire in morality depends on conditions that elude our control.

This has been one of the constant themes of Bernard Williams's writings. But sometimes Williams seems to associate it with a different idea that does not follow from it and that should be guarded against – namely, skepticism toward the very notion of categorically binding obligations.[25] The fact that our interest in morality is empirically conditioned and so subject to luck does not undermine the proposition that certain obligations are ours, whatever our empirically conditioned interests. To believe that it does would equally assume, though in a spirit contrary to Kant's, the strong connection between "ought" and "can" that I have sought to question. We must keep in mind the crucial distinction between scope and motivational basis. The position that must

87

be defended against the twin temptations of postulating a transcendental freedom and denying the categorical nature of certain obligations is one that Kant himself presented in his "precritical" period. His *Lectures on Ethics* of 1775–80 distinguish far more explicitly than his later writings between "the principle of the discrimination of our obligation" (scope) and "the principle of its performance" (motivational basis). And they argue that whereas the understanding discerns that the moral law commands categorically, training and habituation are required to move human beings to fulfill these commands. Here Kant considered the motivational basis of obligation to be a basically empirical matter. He could already complain that the ancient philosophers erred in tailoring their morality to human nature, yet this defense of the categorical imperative (whose first appearance he assigned to the Gospels) led him here, not to a doctrine of transcendental freedom, but rather to the possibility that sometimes divine grace may be necessary.[26]

It is this relative indifference of the content of (universal) morality to moral psychology that is on the track of the truth. The weak connection between obligation and motivation that I outlined earlier shows that the two cannot be detached from one another altogether, as Kant in these lectures believed. But, to a certain extent, it is true to say that our duty is one thing and our state of mind simply another.

An important objection to this view is that it does not correspond to our notions of moral responsibility and to our practices of moral praise and blame. How can we hold someone responsible for not having done what he ought to do, if it was not then in his motivational power to do it? Indeed, Kant believed that our holding everyone responsible for performing his categorical obligations and our blaming anyone who fails to do so shows that we must attribute to everyone an empirically unconditioned ability to do what he ought to do.[27] I do not think, however, that these phenomena require a metaphysical explanation. Our notion of responsibility is not a simple one; it pulls us, in fact, in two different directions, but neither harbors the idea of an empirically unconditioned freedom. Sometimes we are inclined to hold a person responsible for a wrongful action even if he was motivationally incapable of doing what was right. The fact that *he* did it makes him, as the source of the action, responsible for it. This position is mirrored in the legal doctrine of "objective liability," whereby the motivational state of the "average man" serves as the standard for whether certain acts are objects of punishment.[28] Sometimes we lean toward the opposite position that no one can be held responsible for not doing what he was not motivationally able to do. But, even then, the case of someone whose character leaves him motivationally "incapable" of doing what he ought to do does not lead us to suppose he must be transcendentally free to do it. Instead, we may say, precisely, that we shall not blame him for failing to do what he indeed ought to have done. Here the conditions for linking obligation and motivation do not correspond to those connecting responsibility and motivation. I do not know whether these two ideas of responsibility can be brought into some systematic order. But neither offers any real support for Kant's theory of freedom.

The fact that someone has a (universalistic) obligation does not imply, therefore, that he now has a motive (empirical or transcendental) to fulfill it. This should be distinguished from the different view, often confused with it, that knowing what one's obligation is thereby gives one a motive to carry it out.[29] This different view about the relation between knowledge of one's obligations and motivation may well be true. Perhaps it is even impossible (and not just analytically so) that one should sincerely believe that X is what one ought to do, without having the least inclination to do it. I do not wish to dispute this here. But what I have said about the empirical conditioning of motives indicates that we cannot come to know or believe what we morally ought to do, apart from a history of training and socialization. This view, too, was maintained by Aristotle, who did not so much deny that reason can move us to act, as insist that the development of practical reason itself depends on the formation of character.[30]

In this section I have sought to show that the moral phenomena (our deepest moral intuitions and the basic facts of psychology) do not require, as Kant believed, the postulation of a nonempirical motivational interest in morality. Consequently, we do not have the reasons Kant thought we do to place our personal ideal at a certain distance toward empirically conditioned ways of life. This means, in turn, that we do not have to adopt the Kantian interpretation of political neutrality, which makes it an expression of what ought to be our ideal of the person. We can remain, instead, with the modus vivendi interpretation of political neutrality.[31]

All these are reasons why we *need not* follow Kant along his controversial path. The greater metaphysical economy of Aristotle's view of the link between obligation and motivation is also a reason, no doubt, why we *ought not* to follow him. In the next chapter I shall explore some further considerations that count positively against Kant's transcendental perspective.

Chapter 5

Political romanticism

I have distinguished two different views of the relation between the political order and ideals of the person. The first sees the political order as predominantly a modus vivendi, a means of accommodation among individuals having divergent conceptions of the good life. On this model, neutrality can serve as the primary political ideal without playing a similar role outside the political realm in our personal ideals. This system of diversity is opposed by the second view, which I have called expressivism. It requires that the political order express our personal ideal, in the sense that its highest ideal must mirror or coincide with what are in general our deepest commitments. Although there could be other systems of accommodation than that which is based on the neutrality of the state, the modus vivendi model has a direct and easily recognizable affinity to the liberal ideal. Liberalism, however, can also take an expressivist form if, as Kant maintained, our highest personal ideal must be autonomy. Kantian liberalism holds that the neutrality characteristic of the political realm be reflected in the distanced attitude that we should adopt throughout toward empirically conditioned conceptions of the good life.

In Chapters 3 and 4 I have argued for two propositions. First, the liberal ideal of political neutrality can be defended as a modus vivendi – without appeal, that is, to controversial ideals such as personal autonomy. Second, Kant was wrong to believe that liberalism ought to take an expressivist form, for it is not true that a commitment to universalistic morality implies a commitment to the ideal of autonomy. In this chapter I shall turn to the disadvantages of Kantian liberalism, and so the reasons why we ought not to understand liberalism expressivistically. One of these disadvantages is that there are good reasons to think that the critical, distanced posture that autonomy requires ought not to be our paramount personal ideal. Another disadvantage is strategic. Tying liberalism so closely to a controversial personal ideal (whatever its validity) has made liberalism itself needlessly vulnerable. Antiliberals could now attack the ideal of political neutrality by criticizing the ideal of personal autonomy.

This is precisely what occured in German political thought after Kant. The German Romantic movement exploited these two disadvantages, developing a pattern of antiliberal thought that is with us still. Herder, Hegel, and others discerned the limits and the costs of the ideal of autonomy, but they put these criticisms to a less desirable purpose. Their ultimate target became the basic liberal belief that the political order should remain neutral toward different ideals of happiness and self-realization. In brief, their argument was this. Because no one can determine with full autonomy how he shall see the world and what goals he shall pursue, but instead can come to understand himself only through participating in shared traditions and social forms – because in some areas he should not even strive for autonomy, the primary role of the state must be not to sustain a kind of neutrality, but rather to embody and foster some particular conception of the good life. Their political conclusion was thus (what I shall understand as) *communitarianism*.

This is a pattern of argument that was not limited to German Romanticism. It continues to dominate antiliberal thought today, most remarkably perhaps in Michael Sandel's recent and influential critique of Rawls's *Theory of Justice*. The fundamental error of this argument lies in what it continues to share with the Kantian liberalism it attacks. It, too, assumes that the political domain should express the highest personal ideals of its members, and so refuses to envision the possibility that the political realm and other areas of social life may heed different priorities. These antiliberals have reasoned that if our personal ideal should not be so abstract a matter as Kant thought, the political order cannot be made to rest upon a principle of neutrality that abstracts from conceptions of the good life. It is not by accident that the German Romantics failed to grasp the form of social differentiation that characterizes a liberal political order understood as a modus vivendi. Their expressivism stemmed from their reliance upon a simple dichotomy: If a society does not form an organic whole, it is fragmented and anomic. It is indeed this ideal of a whole expressed in each of its parts that shaped the Romantics' vision of both society and the individual. It moved them to demand that a substantial notion of the good unite all areas of social life and that the individual overcome the "alienating" distinction, the *Entzweiung*, between the roles of *homme* and *citoyen*. They could not abide the idea that what is relevant in one domain need not be so in another. They longed for an all-pervading spirit of community that (they imagined) religion had once provided and that a distinction-drawing Enlightenment had dismissed.

I shall proceed by first examining both the valuable criticisms that the German Romantics directed against Kant's ideal of autonomy and the expressivism that led them astray. Then I shall turn to the continuing importance of Romantic ideals for later forms of antiliberalism. After discussing Marx's commitment to Romantic ideals, I shall show how Romantic patterns of argument reappear in antiliberal thought today, its apparent strength largely dependent upon the presence of Kantian elements in the contemporary forms of liberalism it attacks.

More than half of this chapter is historical. But this, I believe, is necessary in order to show how distressingly recurrent and hackneyed is a certain pattern of antiliberal thought.

HERDER: PLURALISM AND EXPRESSIVISM

It was Johann Gottfried Herder, another philosopher from Königsberg, who introduced what became the leading political and social ideas of German Romanticism. Concrete forms of life, in which individuals grow up and with which they identify themselves constitutively, can offer possibilities of self-fulfillment, he insisted, which an attitude of cosmopolitan detachment cannot replace. His great contribution was to point out the costs of pursuing the ideal of a self defined antecedently to shared social forms. His primary target was the egoistic hedonism of Enlightenment *philosophes* such as Helvétius and Holbach. But his criticisms were general enough to extend to Kant's more sublime ideal of personal autonomy, and this was the task pursued by Hegel in his notion of *Sittlichkeit*.

Different from all other animals by reason of their instinctual poverty, we become human, Herder argued, only through participation in society and tradition. We cannot have any significant understanding of ourselves, of what we are and what we ought to be, except by already sharing in common forms of life. Often he expressed this point by saying that thinking is inseparable from the social institution of language, by which he meant the whole way a culture has of understanding the world. The natural state of man is society.[1] Our individuality consists not in how we may remain untouched by socially sedimented patterns of belief and action, manipulating social forms from some position outside them. It has rather to do with how we shape ourselves through developing social forms further in new situations. The extent to which reality may seem to confirm the egoistic hedonist's view of human unsociability depends itself upon given forms into which human beings have been socialized. There is no part of us, Herder believed, that escapes this social formation, not even our moral selves. Our understanding of what morality requires and our commitment to it depend upon empirical conditions. In fact, the *Briefe zu Beförderung der Humanität* contain both a passage where Herder insisted explicitly upon this fact and his well-known encomium of Kant where he endorsed the categorical nature of the moral law.[2] So Herder's understanding of universal morality may not have been far from that which I developed in the preceding chapter.

At its most provocative, Herder's idea of the social formation of the self incorporated two distinct elements. It included, as I have said, a psychological theory according to which our self-understandings always have a social origin, however much we succeed in individualizing them. But it also prescribed a normative constraint on the extent to which we should develop a critical distance toward the social forms that have shaped us. To see what this involved, it should be recognized that even if, contrary to Kant, there is no part of us that is empirically unconditioned, we can still come to put some distance between ourselves and the social forms in which we have grown up. We can slacken our constitutive attachments to them, and thus become willing to accept in imagination a life without them. In this way we might seek to draw ourselves closer to Kant's ideal of autonomy. Now Herder's claim is that the value of thus increasing our autonomy is sharply limited.[3] Detachment toward some social forms (e.g., the business hours in one's own country) is healthy, but extended throughout it becomes ruinous. About this I believe that Herder was importantly right. Shared customs and outlooks involving things of ultimate significance, the ties of place and language, ideas of the good life and morality itself, can lose much of their value, if they do not embody our very idea of the persons we are. That is why our acceptance of them cannot be a matter of decision, as if we had a firm sense of what is valuable apart from them, but must rather be passive, a matter of conviction. "The blurred heart of the indolent cosmopolitan," Herder wrote, "is a shelter for no one. Do we not then see, my brothers, that nature has done everything she could, not to broaden, but to limit us and to accustom us to the circumference of our life."[4] Recognizing the value of constitutive attachments does not preclude our making them the object of critical inquiry, examining their disadvantages and comparing them with other things of value; but it is incompatible with treating them as we (should) treat modern scientific theories, viewing their possible abandonment with equanimity.

Neither autonomy nor belonging can be our paramount goal. We must strive, Herder urged, for the appropriate mix. However, he believed there were also limits to accommodating different values within a single existence. Different forms of life contain valuable, but often mutually unrealizable conceptions of self-realization. The good is inherently heterogeneous. No ideal of the fulfilled life can be pursued except at the price of other valuable possibilities left unexplored. "Ist nicht das Gute auf der Erde *ausgestreut?*"[5] Herder is one of the few thinkers to have recognized, frankly and enthusiastically, the pluralism of ideals of the good and the rich multiplicity of the ways of life embodying them.

This pluralism, along with the critique of cosmopolitan autonomy, are the positive features of Herder's thought. But he did not turn them to a defense of liberalism, combining them instead with an expressivistic idea of state and society. This is because he thought of shared forms of life and constitutive attachments as existing primarily at the level of the whole society. His pluralism fixed chiefly on the variety of societies, and not on diversity within a society. Leaning upon Aristotle's whole/part model of society, he conceptualized societies themselves as expressive or organic wholes, in which common goals animate and harmonize all the different elements of the totality. His enthusiasm for wholeness was all-pervasive, extending to society and the individual alike. Just as the different "faculties" of the mind – sensation, intelligence, imagination – do not function independently of one another, but are together engaged in whatever one does, he argued, so constitutive attachments to a shared form of life tie all the members of society to a single substantial purpose or conception of the good life. Either a society forms an expressive whole or it has collapsed into a heap of indifferent or antagonistic fragments, stripped of any shared bonds of conviction. This is the stark alternative in terms of which Herder philosophized.[6]

As a result, he was of two minds about the view of the

political realm that this expressivistic theory of society required. Sometimes he praised the societies of stateless people, since in them individuals could not be sacrificed to some alien goal. At other times he passionately extolled the worth of the state, so long as, like supposedly the Greek polis, it did express the society's shared conception of the good life: "The most natural state is thus *one* people, with *one* national character."[7] Uniting these two attitudes was Herder's inability or unwillingness to grasp the liberal ideal that the state should have a *specific* function, rationally acceptable to all, but not identical with the important, even constitutive, but generally divergent purposes pursued elsewhere in the society. His social holism kept him from seeing that the political ideal of neutrality toward such constitutive purposes is compatible with their centrality in individuals' personal ideals. The state, for Herder, must be nothing or everything.[8]

To the extent, then, that Herder had a theory of the state, it was an expressivist one. But his was clearly not a political expressivism of the Kantian sort, in which the state is to remain neutral toward substantial conceptions of the good life because it reflects our own autonomous stance toward those conceptions. What separated Herder from expressivist liberalism was his critique of the ideal of autonomy. This part of his thought has much to be said for it. But Herder's error lay in what kept him from a modus vivendi model of liberalism, which can accommodate the importance of constitutive attachments to substantial ideals. His mistake was a fascination with wholeness, his assumption that constitutive ties must extend across all of society to exist at all, his failure to acknowledge the pluralism within society. The result was that he turned his critique of personal autonomy into a rejection of the political ideal of state neutrality.

Shared conceptions of the good life rarely extend throughout the whole of modern societies. But this does not lead to fragmentation. Cooperation is possible among those having different constitutive ideals of the good, different personal ideals, so long as they share the values (rational conversation, equal respect) necessary for a liberal political order. In this way, the demands of one area of social life (e.g., religion) can be kept distinct from those that belong to the political order, so that – although their differentiation embodies a shared value – the beliefs and activities most characteristic of each area will not express a common purpose. Neither "organicness" nor "fragmentation" fits the complex and differentiated societies of modern times.

Herder's thought is paradigmatic for the argumentative style of German Romanticism. A theory of the state's proper functions is based directly, expressivistically, upon a theory of the person that rejects the supremacy of the ideal of autonomous detachment toward empirically conditioned forms of life. The result is abandonment of the liberal ideal of political neutrality. In part Herder influenced and in part he simply anticipated the pattern of German political thought that arose in the wake of the French Revolution. For example, Schiller's *Über Anmut und Würde* (1793) criticized explicitly Kant's exaltation of our moral self above empirical contingencies. The "whole man" or the "schöne Seele," he argued, consists in a full reconciliation of our sense of duty and empirical inclination, and this will come about, not by our making inclination obedient to duty (as Kant demanded), but only by our being able to heed both parts of ourselves harmoniously.[9] This idea of the whole man Schiller then insisted should be directly reflected in the state. His *Briefe über die ästhetische Erziehung des Menschen* (1795) assigned to the state the ennobling function of overcoming the division of labor, amalgamating work and enjoyment, and uniting morality and happiness as only a work of art can do.[10] Once again, the mistake is plain: Wholeness may be a fine personal ideal, but people will differ about the empirical forms needed to realize it, so the state should be not expressive but neutral. Among other Romantics the longing for the organic state was even more unbridled, the resentment toward any separation between *homme* and *citoyen* even more intense. "A great failing of our states," Novalis wrote, "is that we see the state too seldom. The state should be visible everywhere, every man should be obviously a citizen. Could not insignia and uniforms be introduced throughout? Whoever believes such things are insignificant does not understand an essential characteristic of our nature." And Adam Müller announced that nothing human, not even science, can be thought of outside the state and dreamt, "if only the whole man would give himself over to the state, not just his worldly possessions."[11] The Romantics' rediscovery of the importance of belonging did not have to lead to a rejection of liberalism.[12] They went astray by casting their insight in the mold of an organic theory of society, in which each part expresses the essence of the whole. This was an aestheticization of politics, the extension of the originally artistic ideal of the organic to the political realm, as Schiller's and Novalis's appeals to the "aesthetic" and "poetical" state make plain. Such a confusion of realms was the very essence of their thought. The consequences were disastrous. Many of Herder's Romantic successors (although certainly not Schiller) became wholesale opponents of French Revolutionary ideals and missionaries of German nationalism and the Counter-Enlightenment. Eagerly endorsing Burke's *Reflections on the Revolution in France,* they extolled feudal aristocracy and theocracy.[13] Some of them (Müller and Schlegel) worked for Metternich. These German Romantics thus played an important role in the tragic course of German political thought and practice for more than a century. More than they, Herder appreciated the truth of pluralism, but he totally missed its significance within societies. Among the German Romantics, only Hegel thought at Herder's level of sophistication, but he did not escape Herder's mistakes.

HEGEL'S IDEA OF SITTLICHKEIT

The connection that Herder drew between his critique of autonomy and the organic model of society had a deep influence upon Hegel, however much he may have otherwise distanced himself from the Romantic movement.[14] His early enthusiasm for Kantian ethics had already begun to break in the youthful, unpublished *Geist des Christentums* (1797–1800). Like Schiller, he found the Kantian division of the self into legislative and obedient parts a form of internal slavery and sought their true reconciliation through the idea of love.[15] But this was not the sort of anti-Kantian position that shaped Hegel's mature writings. A more fruitful critique of Kant's idea of the empirically unconditioned moral self first appears in Hegel's essay on natural law of 1802–03; it grew in articulation through the later *Rechtsphilosophie* (1821). The guiding thought of this critique was that Kant's ethical theory was too narrowly conceived to appreciate the moral value of institutions, or what Hegel called *Sittlichkeit*.

One way he had of formulating this criticism was not very felicitous. If I steal from someone, Kant had argued, I cannot at the same time will that my maxim become universal law, for that would be to destroy the institution of property of which my maxim aims to take advantage. While granting that Kant's criterion of universalizability can show the immorality of theft, Hegel insisted that it was important to explain why property itself is a valuable institution. Kant, it seemed to him, saw morality simply as a matter of individual agents negotiating their conduct with regard to a given set of institutions that themselves are not subject to moral evaluation.[16]

Strictly construed, Hegel's objection is not quite fair, since the first part of Kant's *Metaphysik der Sitten* sought to provide a moral justification for the various forms of property relations. Nonetheless, Hegel's criticism contains another, more valuable element, which does indicate a decisive way in which Kant ignored the moral significance of institutions. Whenever analyzing the moral worth of institutions, Kant preferred to regard them as constructed (of course, hypothetically) by contracting individuals. This was his approach, whether the institution was marriage or the state.[17] The device of hypothetical contracts yields, however, a one-sided perspective on the relation between morality and institutions. Following Herder, Hegel rightly insisted that the moral worth of institutions can lie, not just in implementing moral commitments that we (or hypothetical agents) already have, but also in encouraging and refining patterns of moral belief and action that might otherwise not exist. The family is the most obvious case of such an institution, and Hegel strenuously resisted Kant's attempt to understand it in contractual terms. But this idea of "institution" also encompasses other social groupings (e.g., churches) as well as shared practices and forms of perception. The important thesis in Hegel's notion of *Sittlichkeit* is, therefore, that institutions not only protect our moral achievements, they also foster moral development. Without socialization into the existing forms of life that embody moral values, individual character would be a thin affair. Commitment to morality involves identifying with its demands so thoroughly that we resist taking seriously the possibility of giving them up. A life without them, we feel, would no longer be recognizable as our own. Not autonomous decision, however, but only training in the given form of life that Hegel called "objective spirit" can establish this bond of conviction. We have a relation to the institutional order, Hegel wrote, that is "more of an identity than even faith or trust."[18]

Kant could ignore this moral role of institutions, of course, precisely because for him thinking of ourselves as moral beings implied viewing ourselves as equipped with an empirically unconditioned sense of duty. Transcendental freedom renders *Sittlichkeit* superfluous. Kant did concede to social forms and institutions the task of removing obstacles: They could mold our empirically conditioned interests into a greater harmony with what we morally ought to do; but they could play no essential role in developing our moral awareness itself. In the previous chapter I showed why we do not need to accept Kant's belief that our sense of duty must be empirically unconditioned. His insight into the categorical nature of universal morality is compatible with Aristotle's more down-to-earth understanding of the relation between obligation and motivation. Hegel had the deepest admiration for Aristotle's ethics, and it is the inseparability of our moral sense from training and socialization that he wanted to bring back to the center of moral theory. His analysis of *Sittlichkeit* offers another persuasive reason, besides that of metaphysical economy (for which Hegel himself had little appreciation), why we should not adopt Kant's transcendental perspective. Moral conviction embodies an inescapable element of passivity, Hegel argued, a constitutive identification with morality's demands, that cannot arise from autonomous decision, but only from the training and socialization that creates our very sense of self.

Hegel's originality lay in the fact that he was the one who brought this Herderian insight to bear against Kant's ethics. He developed it further in the contrast he constructed between *Sittlichkeit* and *Moralität* and in the manner in which he proposed to reconcile them. For Hegel, *Sittlichkeit*, or the recognition that moral character grows out of training in given social forms, had its paradigmatic, if ultimately too narrow, expression in the Greek polis and in classical Athenian moral and political thought. *Moralität*, or the morality of conscience, is the term he used to designate the Kantian position and to include two distinct ideas: the empirically unconditioned nature of the moral self, and the universalist categorical nature of morality. Whereas Kant had seen the closest of links between these two components, Hegel wished to maintain only the latter and this is why *Moralität* was for him an ambivalent phenomenon. Sometimes he denounced the morality of conscience as empty, and then he had in mind the sort of criticisms I have just recounted. At other times he had a far more favorable view of *Moralität* as a distinctively modern attitude, a Christian principle that displaced the polis's constricted reliance upon ethnocentric custom and established the infinite worth of each individual. What we must preserve of *Moralität*, Hegel then was arguing, was its universalistic morality.[19] Dismantling the constellation of *Moralität* in this way allowed Hegel to combine its valuable element with the Aristotelian emphasis upon training and social forms, to reconcile *Moralität* and *Sittlichkeit*, modern and ancient. We must see, Hegel urged, that the central importance of universal morality in our time is sustained and fostered by the institutions and practices characteristic of our society.

This is one of the great ideas of moral and social theory. It inspired my effort in the previous chapter to show, in more analytical detail than Hegel himself, how the insights of Aristotle and Kant can be combined.

It is unfortunate, however, that Hegel's nostalgia for Greece did not stop here. Instead, pursuing the idea of *Sittlichkeit*, but yoking to it an organic model of society, he ended by rejecting the liberal ideal of political neutrality. Institutions and practices, he correctly observed, play a formative role not just in the area of universal morality, but also in the other dimensions of our ideas of happiness and self-fulfillment. Because no part of us, not even our sense of universal morality, transcends such empirical conditioning, there can no longer be the reasons that Kant felt he had for holding that our highest personal ideal must be to maintain a certain distance toward empirically conditioned conceptions of the good life. Our personal ideal does not have to consist in a priority of the right over the good, and particularistic duties, Hegel properly noted, can become central to our self-understandings.[20] But at this point he began to falter. He could not resist the Romantic idea that the state must express our deepest commitments. This is because, like Herder and the other Romantics, he trusted in the conceptual power of the opposition between fragmentation and organic whole, between "alienation" and "reconciliation," "difference" and "identity." Philosophy, Hegel wrote, grows out of the need to overcome alienating divisions *(Entzweiungen)*.[21] If the state is not to be an alien and mechanical power, he insisted, it must have an institutional order that reflects our full self-understanding. For this task the contractarian view of the state as a modus vivendi was, he realized, altogether unsuitable.[22] Instead, he demanded a renewal of the Aristotelian idea that the function of the state lies not simply in protecting property and personal freedoms, but most importantly in fostering and sustaining the ethical substance of its members, which includes not just universal morality but a full conception of the good. The scope of the state should extend beyond abstract justice and take in a whole way of life, a *Volksgeist*, for the Volk is prior to the individual.[23] As in the case of Herder, a rejection of autonomy as the paramount personal ideal, together with a commitment to expressivism, led to the abandonment of political neutrality, and the espousal of a substantial communitarianism.

Hegel did not believe that the state may simply cancel out our individuality. "Subjective freedom," he conceded, is a modern accomplishment, so we cannot reinstate the simple unreflective sort of unity he attributed to the polis. Still, Hegel's ambition was to recreate the polis under modern circumstances. He failed to grasp that it was this aping of the polis that encouraged the terroristic deterioration of the French Revolution, and not the Kantian sort of morality that he oddly attributed to Robespierre and St. Just.[24] The state will respect our individuality, he thought, if it commands an allegiance that is not merely habitual and traditional, but also rationally transparent.[25] Precisely this rational insight is what Hegel wanted his defense of the "ethical state" to bring about. Because the proper task of the state is to embody the *Sittlichkeit* through which we acquire our complete self-understanding, we should venerate the state as a God upon earth.[26]

This divinization of the state has made Hegel appear to many as the apologist of Prussianism.[27] Such criticisms, however, are misdirected. Hegel's topical motives are unclear, and anyway irrelevant. Let us presume that he did not find his ideal of the ethical state fully realized in the Prussia of Friedrich Wilhelm III. The important point is that by breaking with the liberal primacy of the right over the good within the political realm, Hegel's ideal cannot resist Prussianism so firmly as liberalism could. Hegel's argument topples because of the poverty of alternatives with which he thought: Fragmentation and "atomism" is not the sole alternative to a society organized politically around a single complete conception of the good life.[28] The common political principles for social order need not be so substantial. They can consist, instead, in a neutrality toward controversial ideals of happiness and self-fulfillment. It was Hegel's allegiance to an organic model of society that blinded him to the possibility that such liberal neutrality is compatible with persons having constitutive ties to more substantial ideals of the good outside the political realm. Accordingly, it led him to slight the crucial fact that the shared forms of life that sustain substantial ideals of the good need not be society-wide to exist; indeed in a society of modern proportions (instead of the agora-sized polis idolized by Aristotle), a pluralism of ideals is only to be expected. Except for his discussion of the family and a fleeting reference to "corporations" (or guilds that would unite otherwise competing firms), Hegel simply ignored all those *intermediate associations*, those common forms of life we share with restricted groups of others, that generally play the dominant role in our socialization. This neglect of intermediate associations is apparent in the exhaustive distinction he drew between "civil society" – in which, he assumed, individuals pursue only their self-interest – and the state – in which through voting and governmental bureaucracy their communal concerns can come into play – between private egoism and political participation.[29] This way of conceiving the distinction between *homme* and *citoyen* is a common argumentative strategy for exalting the political as the highest form of activity. By assuming that what is private or extra-political comprises only egoistic behavior, this form of thought can easily insinuate that political activity offers the only avenue for truly transcending self-interest. It is an argument that antiliberals have always been happy to exploit, in order to make politics the special domain for deliberating about and pursuing the good life. Liberalism's refusal to grant this special role to politics has thus been seen to lead to social atomism.[30]

However, the premise of this Hegelian argument is patently false. The private realm, as contrasted with the political, does not consist solely in self-interested behavior. This idea that liberalism fosters atomism is a part of a more general misunderstanding that one meets in antiliberal writers. Liberalism, it is often said, is an "individualistic" doctrine: [31] With no room for the constitutive ties that bind persons together in shared forms of life, it makes all social relations "voluntary," in the sense of being extrinsic to the deepest self-understandings of those participating in them. For liberals, however, "individualism" need mean only a *political and legal* doctrine about how people are to be treated in *these* areas of social life. There they are to be treated apart from status and ascription, not as constitutively identified with any roles or groups. Marriage, for example, will then be, for legal purposes, a contractual relation between persons of utterly separate identities, who thus may also divorce; obviously the lived reality of a marriage can be a more mutually entwining bond than this. Such constitutive ties are not for a liberal, however, politically or legally relevant. Liberalism need not include a general recipe for man and society, and it should not pretend to be one, inasmuch as the liberal ideal of political neutrality is a response to the controversiality of personal ideals. It is true, as I have remarked earlier, that liberal writers themselves have not always fully respected this separation of realms. Some like Kant and Mill have urged, in effect, a general sort of individualism. But in this they have run counter to the motivating spirit of liberalism. Hegel's argument, however, showed no real insight into the core of the liberal distinction between "private" and "public." [32]

Like Herder, Hegel rearticulated the value of belonging for our ideals of the good life. Like Herder, too, he succumbed to organic and expressivist views of society and state. Consequently, he too reasoned that if our personal ideal should not be one simply of detachment toward empirically conditioned ideals of the good life, neither can our political ideal be so. But the ideas of belonging and social organicism are not the same, nor logically connected. Their co-presence has made political romanticism an ambivalent phenomenon, possessed of genuine social insights that many contemporaries (and some liberals) had ignored, but misdirected by dangerous political ideals. Organic models of society – the dichotomy between atomistic fragmentation and wholes whose parts are animated by a single, ultimate purpose – have haunted social thought from Aristotle through the German Romantics, from Tönnies's *"Gemeinschaft"* and Lukacs's *"Totalität"* to contemporary "holisms." Aristotle's own formulation of it , the *pars pro toto* variant, according to which one particular part of society (the political) is peculiarly suited to be the site where this common purpose comes to full self-reflective expression, has had too often a stranglehold on political theory, as we will continue to see in the next sections.[33] Meanwhile, sociological theory has elaborated a number of models of social order that are more complex and less brittle than the organic model. There is Hayek's notion of "catallaxy," means-connected systems without a common hierarchy of ultimate ends. There is the similar idea of "functional differentiation," elaborated by sociologists such as Parsons and Luhmann.[34] These are the models of society upon which political theorists should learn to rely.

MARX'S CRITIQUE OF LIBERALISM

Marx did not have a very high estimation of the neutrality to which liberal ideals of justice aspired. In characteristically immoderate fashion he dismissed notions such as "equal right" and "distribution" as "obsolete verbal rubbish."[35] His anger did not fix primarily upon the way in which nineteenth century captialist society may have failed to live up to liberal ideals; he believed, indeed, that capitalism did correspond to its own ideals of justice. Marx believed that these ideals themselves were fundamentally flawed. They were not humanizing, but rather alienating.

Underlying Marx's critique of liberal ideals was the basic element of political romanticism I have already discussed – the cult of wholeness and the repudiation of the separation of social spheres. The division of labor, in both the economic and broader senses, was in Marx's eyes the root of all evil. It is true that he did not strictly have an expressivist theory of the state, since he believed that the state would and ought to wither away. And so he had little of the nostalgia for the Greek polis that has animated romantic antiliberalism from Hegel to Strauss and Arendt (in *The Holy Family* he criticized Robespierre and St. Just for trying to reinstitute Greek political ideals in a modern context).[36] Nonetheless, it was precisely his allegiance to the expressivist ideal that moved him to anarchism. No state is ultimately justifiable, he believed, because no state, no conception of justice, can express the whole man. This conclusion was not unfamiliar to some of the earlier German Romantics as well.[37]

Marx was far less interested in justice than in a certain positive ideal of freedom. People are free, in his view, to the extent that they can unobstructedly develop and exercise their capacities for their own sake. We may call this a self-realization ideal of freedom, so long as we strip the notion of "self-realization" of any reference to a pregiven human essence. Consider the following description of human freedom from the *Grundrisse* (where, as a matter of fact, he is contrasting the expansion of freedom with the closed society of the Greek *polis*):

> The absolute working out of his creative potentialities, with no presupposition other than the previous historic development, which makes this totality of development, i.e., the development of all human powers as such, the end in itself, not as measured on a *predetermined* yardstick.[38]

This is what the full expression of human freedom would supposedly be like under communism. There will exist no pregiven standard to delimit in advance its permissible scope. The limits of human freedom will depend only on the conditions of feasibility that have arisen out of past historical developments. In communist society the material preconditions of freedom will have been so largely satisfied, Marx believed, that the resulting range of freedom will make everything in the past look like mere "prehistory."

This passage, by itself, is doubly ambiguous. First, it is not clear whether the sort of standard to which Marx is referring has to do with justice or with some other value. Secondly, the absence of a *pregiven* standard for judging free activity may mean either that the very idea of judging free activity will be out of place or that the valid standard for such judgments must be one that arises within this new social formation itself. Some of this unclarity disappears, however, in the light of other things that Marx wrote.

Marx had a general reluctance to offer pronouncements about the nature of communist society. Nonetheless, a number of his theoretical commitments did lead him to deny that at least one part of morality – namely justice – would have any role in communism. Under communist conditions, Marx believed, justice will have withered away, along with the state. And thus the realm of freedom, which Marx trusted to flourish under these conditions, was for him an unconditional good, at least in this respect. Of course, since not even socialist society can dispense entirely with economic activity, authority relations essential to the division of labor will continue into the postcapitalist world. Marx did not deny that to some extent the realm of necessity is permanent. But he did believe that these "authority relations" would not contain a conception of justice.[39]

Marx's lack of interest in justice generally depends on his historical materialism. Conceptions of distributive justice, he believed, are *relative* to particular modes of production; in the sense that the conception of justice incorporated in the political state of a given society is one that serves to legitimate the already existing economic formation. Thus, Marx insisted that capitalism was just in the sense of justice typical of capitalist society. The contract between capitalist and worker is a fair and just bargain, he argued, since the capitalist is buying his labor power at the price at which all commodities under capitalism are valued – namely, the socially necessary labor time for producing it.[40] Marx almost never condemned capitalism for being unjust, and this fact alone shows what little weight he gave to conceptions of justice. Consider this general statement from *Capital*:

> To speak here of natural justice, as Gilbart does, is nonsense. The justice of the transaction between agents of production rests on the fact that these arise as natural consequences out of the production relationship. The juristic form in which these economic transactions appear as willful acts of the parties concerned, as expressions of their common will and as contracts that may be enforced by law against some individual party, cannot, being mere forms, determine this content. They merely express it. This content is just whenever it corresponds, is appropriate to the mode of production. It is unjust whenever it contradicts that mode. Slavery on the basis of capitalist production is unjust; likewise fraud in the quality of commodities.[41]

There is no "natural" notion of justice, Marx thought, trans-historically applicable, only relative notions that simply express given modes of production.

Of course, the claim that capitalism is just in the sense of justice appropriate to capitalism ("bourgeois justice") leaves open the possibility that it might appear unjust in the light of some other, superior conception of justice. Marx rejected this possibility, however, precisely because the economic formation that is superior to capitalism would have no need, he believed, of any conception of justice. For Marx there is no such thing as "communist justice." In fact, whatever generally Marx had to say about justice concerned the liberal conception of justice, the paramount concern for equality of formal rights, fair distribution, the separation between *homme* and *citoyen*. And he had special reasons for believing that the liberal concern with justice would wither away. Before examining these reasons, I want to make a few critical observations about Marx's general dismissal of the importance of justice.

Marx's doctrine of the relativity of conceptions of justice forms part of his more general view of the relation between the economic mode of production and the rest of society, between base and super-structure. But it was not merely one application of historical materialism among others. Instead, Marx worked out his materialist theory of history as a generalization of this view of justice. In his preface to *A Contribution to The Critique of Political Economy*, he noted that his first step toward that theory was to realize that legal and political relations grow out of and express the rest of society – what Hegel called "civil society." His next step, of course, was to arrive at the idea that the economic mode of production formed the causally most important part of civil society. Historical materialism arose, therefore, from a prior conviction that justice, as embodied in the law and in the state, possesses no significant autonomy with respect to civil society.[42]

Now the idea that the conception of justice enshrined in the state only expresses the given conditions of civil society is not something at which Marx arrived on his own. On the contrary, it belonged to the core of the historical theory of law developed by von Savigny, whose lectures Marx attended at the University of Berlin. He repudiated his teacher's conservatism, but not this dependence-thesis, which is importantly mistaken, and politically pernicious. Because of this basic axiom, the Marxist theory of the state has always been stunted. It underestimates the crucial ways in which law and the state have reformed civil society.

One clear example of how the relation of dependence may be reversed is the way the sixteenth and seventeenth century state was able to use theories of undivided sovereignty and legal personality to overthrow the dominance of feudal relations.[43] In this regard we should recall that von Savigny's theory of law won wide acceptance in those German circles interested in repudiating the *Code Napoléon* and maintaining Germany's semifeudal conditions; Marx shared a little too much with his political adversaries. Another example, closer to home, is how civil rights legislation has profoundly altered the American way of life; in this case, too, the law had to enforce what civil society by and large was unwilling to grant. There is no denying, of course, that some aspects of the law or the state do express the existing conditions of civil society (and the given mode of production included). And it may be true that no state can successfully reform civil society without the support of some faction of it. But these two concessions do not salvage the von Savigny–Marx thesis that *all* important features of the state or the law reflect the given and *most pervasive* conditions of civil society.

For these reasons, Marx's thesis that the politically empowered conception of justice belongs to the causally dependent superstructure is indefensible. Even less plausible is the general theory of history he elaborated on its basis: Historical materialism exemplifies the *pars pro toto* approach to society that I criticized in the previous section and that I shall not take seriously here.

I shall now turn to Marx's more specific reasons for believing that the liberal conception of justice would disappear under communism. Marx had two separate arguments for this view: The first claiming that liberal justice would be *unnecessary*, the second that it would be *undesirable*. The first rests on mere carelessness, but the second betrays his allegiance to the tradition of political Romanticism.

Capitalist society has been riven, according to Marx, by extensive interpersonal conflicts, one of which sustains all the others – namely, the class struggle. The state exists to contain these conflicts, in part by means of an ideology that presents the ruling class's interest as the general interest. The ideology will include some liberal conception of justice, some way of balancing off the conflicting interests by assigning, in a supposedly neutral way, various rights to different parties. This was Marx's way of putting the idea that justice has a point only as a response to competing claims. But his special point was that under communism this problem will have disappeared, so that there will be no need for a system of justice. He seems to have believed that interpersonal conflicts having society-wide effects stem entirely from two factors that will no longer exist in communist society – systematically distorted beliefs about social reality and egoistic behavior. With the demise of capitalism, Marx supposed, the circumstances of justice, as Hume called them, would have withered away.[44] The expansion of free activity would have no need of being checked by a liberal system of justice.

Marx's argument hangs on an importantly erroneous premise, which he has not been the only one to assume. What makes justice necessary is not egoism per se, but rather competing claims on collectively binding decisions. These claims may express selfish interests or ideas of the general good; it is their variety that matters. Even if in a classless society all people genuinely pursue the general interest, with their minds clear of ideological distortion by particularistic interests, their ideas of the general interest will probably not coincide. Universal benevolence does not guarantee universal agreement. We can imagine that in a classless society rival groups could form around different disinterested conceptions of the general good. Thus, as I observed in the previous chapter, the circumstances of justice are not exhausted by ignorance and limited altruism. A classless society will still have to make collectively binding decisions about competing conceptions of the general good, and so it will have need of a state and of conceptions of justice to adjudicate these disputes.[45] In fact, communism as Marx foresaw it would make a system of justice, and in particular a liberal conception of justice, more central than ever before. The less we think in ideologically routinized ways, and the more we freely exercise our powers and cultivate our individuality, the more various and divergent will be our conceptions of the good life. Greater freedom means greater variety, a deeper recognition of pluralism, and a stronger need for toleration; so all the more must we ensure that the liberal conception of justice is the primary value of our political institutions. Marx was wrong to believe that the pursuit of freedom, the value he seems to have held paramount, would render justice otiose. The government of persons cannot be replaced simply by the administration of things.

Marx's second argument against liberal justice was differently aimed. Not only dispensable, he believed it is also undesirable. The pattern of this argument is the one we have seen to be the essence of political romanticism. Marx appealed to the notion of the "whole man," not simply as a personal ideal whose validity is established outside the political realm, but rather as an ideal that would overcome the liberal differentiation between the political and the nonpolitical. Schiller's letters, *Über die ästhetische Erziehung des Menschen*, had offered the canonical exposition of this combination of individual wholeness and political expressivism. Equally influential upon Marx were the writings of Rousseau, who had lamented the modern differentiation between *homme* and *citoyen*, the private and the public. "Toutes les institutions qui mettent l'homme en contradiction avec lui-même ne valent rien."[46] Our aim must be to lead lives all of whose aspects are animated by a common purpose, instead of having different parts specialized to different ends.

This ideal of the whole man already permeates Marx's early writings. Both the *Critique of Hegel's Philosophy of Right* and *On The Jewish Question* equate modernity with the distinction between the private and the public, civil society and the state, and long for its *Aufhebung*:

> The abstraction of the state as such belongs only to modern times because the abstraction of private life belongs only to modern times. The abstraction of the political state is a modern product.... Human emancipation will only be complete when the real, individual man has absorbed into himself the abstract citizen; when as an individual man, in his everyday life, in his work, and in his relationships, he has become a *species-being;* and when he has recognized and organized his own powers *(force propres)* as *social* powers so that he no longer separates this social power from himself as political power.[47]

Marx never lost his distaste for the social separation of spheres. In general, he had nothing but contempt for the civil freedoms that set the limits of governmental intervention in social life. Such negative or "formal" freedom, as he called it, seemed to him mostly a capitalist ruse, and he tended to consider his own positive notion of freedom as a *substitute* for it, and not as a *complement* of it; not, that is, as simply a personal ideal. The sole way in which he might seem to differ here from the Romantics was his conviction that the state would wither away. But even such anarchism was not foreign to Romantic expressivism, for which, as we saw in the case of Herder, the state should be either everything or nothing, but never something of an only specific relevance. Marx shared the Romantics' hatred for the institutionalized myopia, for the distinction between what is relevant in a certain context and what is not, which political liberalism demands. Marx wanted the state to disappear, precisely because he believed that no state could express the whole man.

Nowhere is this clearer than in one of Marx's later writings, the "Critique of the Gotha Programme" (1875). There he appealed in effect to the ideal of the whole man in order to dismiss the idea that socialism will carry out a just distribution of tasks and resources. At the initial stage of communism, Marx claimed, resources will be distributed on the basis of labor-value contributed. However, this principle of distribution remains one of "bourgeois right," since it applies an equal standard – an "exchange of equivalents" – to each according to his labor. Marx observed that

> one man is superior to another physically or mentally and so supplies more labor in the same time, or can labor for a longer time; and labor to serve as a measure, must be defined by its duration or intensity, otherwise it ceases to be a standard of measurement. This *equal* right is an unequal right for unequal labor.[48]

Marx seems clearly to have supposed that his argument is a perfectly general one. *Any* standard of equality will have the same result: "It is, therefore, a right of inequality, in its content, like every right." Any standard that treats men equally in a respect where they are the same will thereby treat them differently (or unequally) in those aspects where they differ. What, we may ask, is so bad about that? The rest of the passage gives the answer:

Right by its very nature can consist only in the application of an equal standard; but, unequal individuals (and they would not be different individuals if they were not unequal) are measurable only by an equal standard insofar as they are brought under an equal point of view, are taken from one *definite* side only, for instance, in the present case, are regarded *only as workers* and nothing more is seen in them, everything else being ignored.

Marx's assumption is that free activity will increase the individuality, the dissimilarity, of different individuals.[49] The resulting pluralism will no doubt extend to their conceptions of the general interest, with consequences – apparently unforeseen by Marx – that I have already noted. But Marx was rather clear that it is not the manifold differences among individuals that led him here to spurn standards of equality. There is no difficulty in treating things the same if we leave out their differences. Instead, he repudiated such standards because inevitably they will fix on just one aspect of individual lives, while neglecting all the others. Standards of equality institutionalize myopia, since in the respects they ignore they treat men differently, unequally. They differentiate the social world into what is politically relevant and what is not. They divide between *citoyen* and *homme*, in the way that the Romantic ideal of the whole man meant to overcome.

Curiously, "The Critique of the Gotha Programme" suggests that the later stage of communism will solve the distribution problem by means of Louis Blanc's principle, "from each according to his ability, to each according to his needs." This solution cannot escape, however, the Romantic objection that Marx lodged against "bourgeois" standards of equality.[50] Let us leave aside the question whether collective decisions might be needed for *which* needs are to be met and by *how much*; such decisions call for some standard of equality for scheduling need satisfaction, but perhaps they would not be necessary if scarcity had been sufficiently conquered. The fact remains that the first part of Marx's formula – "from each according to his ability" – is quite obviously a standard of equality, which in other respects treats different men differently (i.e., unequally). If it means that everyone, whatever his task, is to perform socially necessary labor for the same amount of time (whatever his productivity), then some will find their working hours more tiring than others. If it means that different tasks will have different mandatory hours, inversely proportional to their strenuousness, then some people will have more free time than others. If there is to be a rotation among different tasks, those who are more readily adaptive will find it easier going. And so on. However construed, this part of Marx's principle is a standard that treats men as equal in one respect, while treating them differentially in the other respects it ignores. So it institutionalizes a distinction between what it deems relevant, and what it does not, between *citoyen* and *homme.* It is difficult to see how any solution to the distribution problem for tasks could do otherwise.

None of this is meant to constitute a criticism of Louis Blanc's recipe for distributive justice. Perhaps it does offer the best means for fostering free individuality. What is certainly wrong, however, is Marx's suggestion that somehow it will escape what displeased him so much in principles of justice: As a standard of equality, it is at the same time (in other respects) a principle of inequality and, thus, a principle for *differentiating* instead of *unifying* the individual. Communist society will have distribution problems to solve, and any egalitarian solution must shove aside the Romantic ideal of wholeness.

Thus, neither of Marx's reasons for dismissing the importance of the liberal conception of justice carries any weight. Enhancement of the prospects for freedom is a noble ideal, but it cannot be pursued apart from the acknowledgment that free individuals are likely to diverge in their conceptions of the good life and that their differences make egalitarianism (in whatever specific form) incompatible with ideals of wholeness. Marx's error was a fatal one. The political horror that institutionalized Marxism has become is not unconnected with Marx's own scorn for the liberal idea of justice.

RAWLS'S AMBIGUITIES AND NEO-ROMANTICISM

Political romanticism thrives off a confusion of realms. Romantics from Herder and Hegel to Marx attacked liberal neutrality for failing to express what ought to be our full self-understandings. Yet the motivating spirit of liberal neutrality has been precisely to prescind from the inherent controversiality of ideals of the person, and to cast political principles in a more abstract form. Liberalism, so understood, is a theory of politics, not a theory of man, and so the Romantic critiques have been misconceived. The situation, however, is not so simple as this. Too often liberals have themselves failed to respect the purely political relevance of neutrality toward conceptions of the good life and personal ideals. Instead, they have urged that in general we sustain a sort of distance toward empirically conditioned ideals, that all social relations be "voluntary" and not constitutive of our deepest self-understandings. Kant's doctrine of autonomy offers the most pellucid example of this tactic (but there is also Mill's personal ideal of experimentalism). This form of argument has exposed liberalism to just the sort of controversiality from which it has sought to escape. The link it established between political and personal ideals allowed the Romantic critique of political neutrality to enjoy an apparent plausibility that this antiliberalism does not really possess.

In the preceding sections I have agreed with much of the Romantic objections to the thesis that autonomy and distance toward traditions and substantial forms of life should be our dominant commitment. We have good reason, I believe, not to make Kantian autonomy our personal ideal. But such beliefs about the nature of the good life are not exactly the *political* form in which I want to put my disagreement with Kant's formulation of liberalism. What is politically relevant is that the value of autonomy is, at least, an object of rational dispute, and so it ought not to serve as a basis for political liberalism. I have defended my own convictions about the good in the hope of reinforcing this point.

I sympathize with the Romantics' recognition of the importance of belonging, but not, of course, with their attack upon political neutrality and the liberal separation of domains. Their expressivistic parallelization of substantial personal and political ideals was often merely automatic and unthinking; at best it rested upon the simplistic dichotomy between organic whole and fragmented anomie. (By contrast, Kant's argument for liberal expressivism – namely, that a commitment to universal morality requires a commitment to personal autonomy – was far more subtle, even if incorrect). Romantic political theory, however influential, has little cogency.

Hegel was the only Romantic to work out a systematic critique of Kantian liberalism. His "reconciliation" (*Versöhnung*) of personal and political ideals is thus the paradigm of political romanticism. His form of argument (if not, thankfully, his form of expression) continues today to nourish antiliberal thought. It has always been a mainstay of the Right, from the beginning intimately connected with the Restoration. Surprisingly, and discouragingly, it finds an increasing resonance among writers situating themselves on the Left.[51] The most important reason for its apparent vitality is that too often liberal thinkers themselves continue to assume the same unnecessary burdens that Kant bequeathed. Kantian ideals of the person, which seek to free the deepest strands of our self-understanding from the web of natural and social circumstance, still exert a powerful attraction upon liberal thinkers.

John Rawls's *A Theory of Justice*, certainly the greatest contribution to liberal theory in our century, did not entirely escape this temptation. Nor did many of its commentators and supporters. As a result, this book has yielded a foothold to a number of recent attacks upon political liberalism, offering little that cannot be found in Hegel except a greater accessibility. In this section I shall examine the ambiguities of Rawls's relation to Kant as well as the corresponding rebirth of antiliberal expressivism in contemporary thought. (I shall assume that the main outlines of Rawls's argument are known, although I shall also discuss how I think some of his central concepts, such as "the veil of ignorance," ought to be understood.)

A Kantian ideal of the person appears a number of times in *A Theory of Justice.* In order to conceive of the right as prior to the good in the political realm, Rawls claims, we must understand that "the self is prior to the ends which are affirmed by it."[52] The political order can maintain a neutrality toward different conceptions of the good life, it seems, only if we understand ourselves as having a certain distance toward them. Our highest personal ideal must be to exercise this capacity for freedom and distance, ensuring that our conception of the good life be a "contingent" one in a special sense: Although natural and social conditions out of our control play an ineliminable role in making it ours, we ourselves should give it the value it has for us. This is what Rawls himself calls "the Kantian interpretation" of his theory of justice.[53] "The desire to express our nature as a free and equal rational being," Rawls writes, "can be fulfilled only by acting on the principles of right and justice as having first priority."[54] Thus, the priority of the right over the good seems no longer simply the fundamental feature of the political order; it should be equally fundamental, Rawls appears to be saying, in our general ideal of the person. This is Kantian expressivism.

Refurbishing Kant's theory of autonomy, however, ran counter to some of Rawls's other and deepest intentions. Both in *A Theory of Justice* and in some of his later writings, he has described his project as delivering Kantian ethics from the metaphysics of transcendental idealism.[55] The fundamental approach of *A Theory of Justice* is to focus upon the Humean "circumstances of justice," to determine what principles of cooperation can be accepted by rational agents whose conceptions of the good life diverge and conflict. If he had held fast to this view of neutral justice as a modus vivendi, Rawls could have allowed for a more concrete ideal of the person. He could have accorded the priority of the right over the good, or the neutrality toward ideals of the good life, a strictly political relevance, governing our role as citizens, without its having to be our dominant ideal in other areas of social life.

But *A Theory of Justice* (as well as some of Rawls's later writings) is not all of one piece. Its liberalism contains both modus vivendi and expressivist strands. It is not surprising, therefore, that contemporary antiliberals have homed in on the more vulnerable expressivist components of this book. They have dressed up the weaknesses in the Kantian ideal of the person as a critique of liberalism itself. In this they have shown only a limited originality, repeating in effect the German Romantic critique of Kant. They continue to share with their Kantian adversary precisely the questionable premise that separates the Kantian perspective from the spirit of classical liberalism – namely, the expressivism that supposes that the highest ideals of the political order must mirror what are our highest personal ideals. From the plausible view that we should not place our deepest personal commitment in an impartiality toward conceptions of the good life, that instead we must see ourselves as constituted by some such conception, they have inferred that the political order must be organized, not around principles of neutrality, but around some unifying vision of the good life.

The most lucid and the most influential of these antiliberal attacks upon Rawls's Kantianism has been Michael Sandel's *Liberalism and The Limits of Justice*. Sandel correctly understands that Rawls's political theory belongs to the great liberal tradition. It locates the primary ideal of the political order in the neutrality of the state and so in an "abstract" conception of justice. The distribution of political and economic benefits is to be regulated by principles that do not presuppose, for their justification, any particular conception of the good life. In this sense the liberal ideal of the primacy of abstract justice makes the right prior to the good.[56] Like his predecessors in the German Counter-Enlightenment, Sandel presents a critique of this ideal that is of a special sort. He largely skirts the unwelcome consequences of liberal politics, and gives little content to the alternative that he favors so that the advantages and drawbacks of the two might be compared. Instead, his concern lies with the weaknesses of the Kantian form of justification that, he argues, dominates Rawls's work. He contends that this Kantian basis can justify the primacy of abstract justice only by appealing to an unacceptable ideal of the person as disencumbered of natural and social circumstance and so prior to its ends and values.

Sandel offers two arguments for why an underlying Kantian ideal of the person makes Rawls's theory of justice unacceptable. The first is a direct attack upon the plausibility of that ideal. Sandel maintains that purifying the self of all those features dependent on natural and social circumstance, so that it may then confer value upon them, amounts to emptying it of all content whatsoever.[57] We could attribute to this disencumbered self a capacity for moral responsibility, only if with Kant we believed that the person has an empirically unconditioned sense of duty. But Kantian metaphysics of this sort, Sandel observes, is what Rawls set out to avoid.[58] He also argues that conceiving of personhood along the lines of a self prior to its ends ignores the phenomena of character and of the intersubjective constitution of the self. By this he means that beyond obligations voluntarily incurred and those owed to human beings as such, many of us have constitutive attachments to particular visions of the good life, which we may share with others. These are not valuable because we freely choose them, as the individualistic Kantian model would urge, for they are "inseparable from understanding ourselves as the particular persons we are." Without them we lack "character" and "moral depth."[59] Sandel's discussion of character is not always as clear as one might wish. This is because he does not distinguish sharply between our being *unable* to conceive of ourselves without some commitment, and our being *unwilling* to do so. Character has to do only with the latter: It consists not in an incapacity of thought, but rather in the refusal to take certain possibilities seriously. But despite this imprecision, Sandel is right to say that we should not let ourselves be bullied by Kantians into thinking that our deepest self-understandings must lie prior to any vision of the good life, which may be embodied in a form of life shared with others. This was one of the important truths contained in Hegel's appeals to *Sittlichkeit*.[60]

But he has not thereby shown that Rawls's principles of justice lack an adequate foundation. This is because Sandel assumes along with Rawls's Kantian interpretation an expressivist model of the political order: The only way an ideal of what we should be as persons can be connected with a conception of the political order, he supposes, is that it mirror the primary ideals of that order. Principles of justice that presuppose no particular conception of the good entail, he believes, that in general we locate our deepest commitments or "self-understandings" antecedent to any particular conception of the good.[61] That is why he assumes that a refutation of this Kantian ideal of the person automatically undermines liberalism, or the political primacy of neutrality and abstract justice. Once we recognize that our personhood must be in part constituted by a commitment to some conception of the good life, he argues,[62] we will grasp that the political order, too, must subordinate justice to that higher, more substantive ideal. Thus, Sandel assumes that we must choose between Kantianism and some form of communitarianism.

He never, however, considers the obvious alternative to the *expressivist* model underlying both these options, one which, I have argued, has a special affinity to the liberal ideal. From the toleration theories of Locke and Bayle, through Hume's theory of justice and nineteenth century theories of the *Staat-Gesellschaft* distinction, many liberals have seen the political system as chiefly a modus vivendi among people having different ultimate commitments (often at home in different subcommunities), a system of mutual advantage, our adherence to which requires that we abstract from controversial ideals of the good life, but in the political domain only, and not in general. Liberalism, so understood, divides social life into different domains of relevancies. Stressing the heterogeneity of the "public" (political) and the "private" (*citoyen* and *homme*), this view is peculiarly suited to modern pluralistic societies, in which there is no general agreement about ideals of the person.

By ignoring this alternative, Sandel, like the German Romantics, can suggest that liberalism is in far greater trouble than it actually is. The modus vivendi view, in fact, forms the other strand in Rawls's *A Theory of Justice*, figuring most prominently in the way he links the principles of justice to the "circumstances of justice."[63] Where interests and conceptions of the good life conflict, Rawls argues, fair principles of justice are those that rational agents would choose in the "original position" behind a "veil of ignorance," where, that is, they could not appeal to those views that divide them. It is not necessary that we see this separation of the person from his conception of the good as itself representing an ideal of the person, a self prior to the ends that it chooses.[64] That is the Kantian interpretation of the original position. But the modus vivendi view of justice offers a different and more economical rationale. As I argued earlier, a general feature of rational discussion is that when parties disagree about how to solve some problem (e.g., what common political principles to institute), they retreat to a common ground, to the views they continue to share despite their differences, with the hope that this common basis either will provide the means for resolving the disagreement one way or the other or at least will yield some neutral principles for solving the ulterior problem they continue to face. The veil of ignorance in Rawls's theory need be taken as no more than just such a common ground. Since modern, pluralistic societies cannot expect general agreement about the nature of the good life, the veil of ignorance will serve not as a basis for arriving at the truth about the good, but rather as a means for devising principles of politicial cooperation that are neutral with respect to the conflicting conceptions of the good.[65] Responding in this way to the circumstances of justice does require that everyone already share some values – namely, rational conversation and equal respect. I indicated earlier, however, that these commitments are largely neutral with regard to ideals of the good. The modus vivendi perspective shows, therefore, how unproblematic it is to understand why *we* should be bound by the principles that *hypothetical* agents in the original position would have chosen – a question that many of Rawls's critics have deemed insoluble.[66] The original position can simply be construed as the neutral ground from which *we* should reason, if we respond to disagreement about the good life with a commitment to rational conversation and equal respect.

A Theory of Justice harbors, side by side, the Kantian and the modus vivendi approaches. Rawls's later writings, and particularly his "Dewey Lectures," have put the second approach in the center where it belongs. These lectures distinguish sharply between how we understand ourselves as citizens within the political system and how we may regard ourselves in our personal affairs or within certain intermediate associations. Citizens, Rawls writes, "do not view themselves as inevitably tied to the pursuit of the particular conception of the good and its final ends which they espouse at any given time."[67] This does not mean that our highest personal ideal must be to conceive of ourselves as prior to our ends, without any constitutive attachment to a conception of the good. It means, instead, that the political system *treats* persons as not necessarily tied to any particular conception of the good, that is, apart from status and ascription. My legal privileges, for example, remain the same even should I convert from one religion to another or refuse any faith. Outside the political realm, however, things may be different. There, as Rawls notes, people "may have attachments and loves that they believe they would not, or could not, stand apart from."[68] This is the difference between *citoyen* and *homme* that liberalism promotes as a sort of institutionalized myopia, and only the modus vivendi conception of justice makes it intelligible.

Sandel's discussion of the circumstances of justice is the closest he gets to glimpsing the alternative to expressivism. But it is a lost opportunity. Connecting the primacy of abstract justice with these empirical circumstances, he claims, is to deny that it is unconditionally valid.[69] This is true, but beside the point. Relative material scarcity, limited altruism, and conflicting conceptions of the good life are, however empirical, also universal features of the human condition. Sandel's objection turns on the fallacy that if something is "empirical," there is some serious possibility it could be different. Thus, against Rawls's more recent anti-expressivist claim in the "Dewey Lectures" that in our personal affairs we can have an unshakable attachment to some idea of the good life, while at the same time the political realm treats us as citizens in abstraction from that, Sandel can reply only that "allowing constitutive possiblities where 'private' ends are at stake would seem unavoidably to allow at least the possibility that 'public' ends could be constitutive as well."[70] True, as an empirical fact the absence of a society-wide consensus about the good life "could" (logically) change. But, short of coercion, it is not about to do so. Outside the political realm, of course, among friends or family or in certain intermediate associations, there can be a shared view of the good life to which considerations of justice may be subordinated. Liberalism, as I have frequently pointed out, does not require an individualistic image of man; its individualism can be strictly political. Sandel, however, seems to prefer the fantasy that society as a whole once was or might become a family or a club of friends.[71] He thus dips into those organic models of society that have always charmed antiliberal writers on the Right, such as Roger Scruton and George Will today.[72] Sandel insists, for example, that fostering abstract justice as the primary political virtue may sacrifice existing sentiments of general benevolence or fraternity. Although formally correct, this point is historically irrelevant, since nonliberal societies, past and present, have scarcely been an idyll of fellow-feeling.

In general, then, Sandel assumes that liberals cannot safely affirm the primacy of abstract justice while appealing to empirical conditions that make it necessary. Not even Kant believed that. Contrary to Sandel, he too connected the primacy of justice with an account of the empirical (though universal) circumstances that require it.[73] In Kant's case, Sandel has failed to distinguish between empirically conditioned motives and responses to empirically conditioned problems.

Sandel's second argument is that Rawls's difference principle (social and economic inequalities are to be arranged so that they are to the greatest benefit of the least advantaged) cannot be convincing unless the Kantian ideal of the person is given up. Rawls himself sought to justify the difference principle by appealing to that ideal in the following way. The function of principles of justice is to determine what people deserve; there is no such thing as desert antecedent to such principles. The distributive principles underlying the ideals of "natural liberty" (careers open to talents) and "liberal equality" (fairness of opportunity as well) hold that people deserve whatever their natural or socially conditioned assets enable them to acquire. Sandel points out that in order to show why we should prefer the difference priniple to these other two principles, Rawls struck a Kantian stance.[74] The person, as the subject of desert, cannot be identified with his naturally or socially conditioned assets, for having these capacities and talents was not altogether under his control and such contingencies cannot belong intrinsically to a self located prior to its ends. Thus, a person cannot automatically deserve the benefits deriving from his assets, so we might better think of them, Rawls concluded, as assets common to us all and ensure that they benefit us all. This is what the difference principle brings about.

Sandel's objection to this reasoning is twofold. First, he leans on Nozick's point that from the premise that an individual does not automatically deserve the benefits of his assets, it does not follow that they should count as common assets.[75] After all, we do not – as a community – have these capacities under our control in the way in which as separate individuals we do not. Second, he points out that they could count as common assets if we no longer distinguished so sharply between ourselves and both our capacities and our ties to others. To do this, we must regard ourselves not as disencumbered selves, but as persons constituted at least in part by some conception of the good life that we share with the other members of our community. To this extent, however, the good will be, after all, prior to the right; and so, Sandel concludes, liberalism represents a flawed and incomplete ideal.[76]

Unfortunately, Sandel overestimates the force of this argument. At most he has shown that *one* rationale for a program (the modern welfare state) that *some* liberals have embraced can succeed only by being inconsistent with a thorough adherence to the primacy of abstract justice. Liberalism does not require welfarism, and there may be other arguments for the difference principle besides the Rawlsian one that Sandel examines. Furthermore, the communitarian argument he proposes for the difference principle is not likely to work. Those people to whom our constitutive ties are strongest, those with whom our own self-understanding is most closely associated, will probably form a rather circumscribed group, fused by some particular conception of the good. In modern pluralistic societies our deepest group allegiances are not apt to extend across the whole society. The aim of the modern welfare state, however, has been to redistribute income and resources precisely on a society-wide basis, taxing some for the benefit of others whether or not they have the same ultimate aspirations. This means that its aim has been to counteract the effects of "constitutive attachments," on which Sandel lays such emphasis. His argument might suffice to defend the taxation of some Catholics for the benefit of other Catholics, or of some blacks for the benefit of other blacks. But how could it justify, for example, redistributing income from Scarsdale to Harlem?

It seems that both Rawls's use of a Kantian ideal of the person and Sandel's appeal to the person as "thick with traits" fail to support the difference principle. This suggests that if we want to hold on to this principle, we discard the assumption that their different arguments share – namely, that this principle must express our deepest personal ideals. A more promising approach might be to base the neutrality of this principle on more purely political considerations, as I suggested earlier in Chapter 3. Everyone agrees that the state must play some role in regulating the distribution of wealth, and so such intervention must be neutral with regard to the interests of rich and poor. Whether this will suffice to ground the difference principle, of course, is a more complex question, involving both normative and economic considerations. My aim is not to answer it here (indeed, it is rightly controversial whether this particular welfarist principle should be upheld, and the answer may be negative). My aim is to indicate how the question should best be discussed.

The real value of Sandel's book, like that of political romanticism in general, lies at cross-purposes to its intent. He has shown not that liberalism is problematic, but at most that liberalism construed expressivistically is so. The Kantian ideal of the person is indeed a controversial one, so we would be unwise to rest our political ideals on so shaky a foundation. However, just this point belongs at the core of the liberal tradition: Conceptions of what we should be as persons are an enduring object of dispute, toward which the political order should try to remain neutral. We do better to recognize that liberalism is not a philosophy of man, but a philosophy of politics.

This means that we must adopt a more positive attitude toward the liberal "separation of domains" than either political romantics or some liberals themselves have shown. From what is of the greatest importance in one domain of social life, we must learn to abstract in another. Liberals such as Kant and Mill, who have coupled their political theory with a corresponding notion of what in general ought to be our personal ideal, have betrayed in fact the liberal spirit. They have thereby exposed liberalism to the "demystification" practiced by antiliberal critics. The fundamental liberal insight is the inescapable controversiality of ideals of the good life and thus the need to find political principles that abstract from them. For this reason, the toleration theories of Bodin, Locke, and Bayle offer a surer model of what political liberalism ought to be like than many of their eighteenth and nineteenth century successors. They recognized that people may have constitutive ties to different ideals of personal salvation and still sustain a political modus vivendi with one another.[77] It is also true, however, that liberalism, so understood, must be combined with a greater commitment to *democracy*, to political participation by all, than any of these three thinkers (except, perhaps, for Locke) displayed, if it is to have this paradigmatic role. But the ideal of liberal democracy does not require any relaxing of the commitment to political neutrality. It does not depend upon assuming that political participation forms a necessary ingredient of any conception of the good life, as those struck with nostalgia for the polis often suppose. Democratic participation can be more economically defended as the best means (when it is so!) for ensuring that the state does remain neutral toward the intrinsic worth of all ideals of the good life.[78] (This neutral justification of democracy does not preclude, of course, that some may indeed find their self-fulfillment in political activity.)

If even liberals have sometimes misunderstood their own fundamental motivation, the liberal separation of realms must apparently be a difficult view to accept fully. The main obstacle has been the organic model of society and, corresponding to this on a more philosophical level, an oversimplified monistic conception of practical reason. Liberalism, properly understood, exemplifies one dimension on which the unity of practical reason must be rejected. We must recognize that practical reason encompasses a number of domain-specific *specializations*.

In the next chapter I shall explore another dimension of moral complexity that I have mentioned several times already – the heterogeneity of morality.

Chapter 6

The heterogeneity of morality

In this chapter I shall examine a dimension of moral complexity that bears on the relation between morality and religion. But I shall not be concerned with the problem with which that relation is usually associated – the objectivity of moral beliefs. If God does not exist, I believe it does not follow that everything is permitted. The idea that only the existence of God can support the objectivity of morals relies upon the dubious epistemology of foundationalism, transposed to the realm of morality. It supposes that our moral beliefs can lay claim to objectivity only if we can show how they can be justified *as a whole*, that this justification en masse is possible only if they are seen to promote some purpose that is ours whether or not we recognize it to be so, and that such a telos can be ours only if there is a God who has created us to that end.[1] The underlying assumption of this outlook is that the *contextual* justification of moral beliefs cannot secure their objectivity. I have argued earlier in this book that such an assumption is baseless and that we have no good reason to deny objectivity to morals in just the sense that we affirm it of science.

However, my concern now will not be with the objectivity of morals, but rather with a problem whose full force depends on granting their objectivity. If we think of a principle of practical reason as a rule for organizing and ranking particular desires or courses of action in the light of some general kind of practical value, then we seem to find ourselves subject to not one, but three such principles, and these principles seem to make contrary demands of us in various situations. Consequently, we can be caught in conflicts between equally objective practical demands: We can confront tragic choices.

These three principles are partiality, consequentialism, and deontology, so they lie at a high level of generality.[2] The principle of partiality underlies what I distinguished earlier (in Chapter 4) as "particularistic" duties. This principle covers those obligations we have only in virtue of some empirically conditioned desire that we also have. For example, partiality requires that we show an overriding concern for the interests of those who stand to us in some particular relation of affection. There are, for example, the duties of friendship and the demands that stem from our participation in some concrete way of life or institution, to protect and foster it. There are also the obligations that arise from more abstract commitments, as when we speak of an artist's duty to his art. In general, the obligations supported by this principle are not "impartial," in the sense that they are not categorical: They apply not independently of one's empirically conditioned desires, but only in virtue of them. The principle of partiality thus expresses a priority of the good over the right. The duties that it encompasses arise from the commitment to some substantial ideal of the good life. The other two principles are universalistic and support categorical obligations. The principle of consequentialism requires that we do whatever will produce the most good or the least evil overall, with regard to all those touched by our action (utilitarianism is the best-known form of this principle). The principle of deontology requires that we never do things of a certain sort to another (break a promise, tell an untruth, kill an innocent person), even if thereby less good or greater evil comes about. Later I shall explain more precisely how these two principles ought to be distinguished (and why some of the usual ways of distinguishing them will not work).

I believe that every reflective person recognizes to some extent the demands of these principles. They are all moral principles, the second two clearly so, and the principle of partiality as well, to the extent that it underlies what Bradley called "my station and its duties." In any case, all three are principles of practical reason in that we understand their general authoritativeness for our decisions. Moreover, they seem to urge *independent* claims upon us: We do not believe, or not without the aid of some sophisticated theory, that one has its validity by being a means to promoting another. They seem to represent independent sources of moral value. Yet clearly their injunctions seem to diverge in particular circumstances. So an important question for ethical theory is how we should regard and resolve the conflicts between such sorts of reasons.[3]

In this chapter I shall focus my discussion of these three principles upon the *extrapolitical* realm. This is because a liberal political order decisively narrows the extent to which, within its boundaries, all three principles can come into play. There the ideal of neutrality must always take precedence over disputed ideals of the good life. Thus, in this area of social life, neutrally justifiable principles of justice (whether deontological or consequentialist in form) must always rank higher than the principle of partiality. Outside the political domain, however, things are not so neat. I argued earlier that without the Kantian personal ideal of autonomy, there seems no reason why here universalistic duties must always outweigh particularistic ones. So my reason for looking chiefly at the extrapolitical realm is that it displays more fully this dimension of moral complexity. Conflicts between deontological and consequentialist duties can figure, however, within a liberal political order, since duties of these sorts need not depend upon controversial ideals of the good life. To this extent liberals will have to recognize that the principle of neutrality will not solve every political problem and that such conflicts may even prove rationally irresoluble.

I shall begin by looking at the exemplary way in which Bishop Butler discussed these three principles. Assigning religion the task of settling their conflicts, Butler's ethical writings thus serve to underscore the difficulty of the problem once we can no longer count on an omnipotent and benevolent God. I shall then examine in some systematic detail the structure of these practical principles and the reason why they conflict.

BUTLER'S PROBLEM

According to Bishop Butler, human nature is a "system." Not only does it consist of distinct components, but the character of some of these is to lay claim to the governance of others. Particular affections are desires for some external object. The principle of self-love ranks these in the light of what will best promote our own happiness. The principle of benevolence orders them in accord with what will best promote the happiness of others, and, unless qualified, this will be the general happiness. Now the authority of a principle must be distinguished from its motivational strength. Even if motivationally weak, the principle of self-love embodies a claim to govern the desire of some external object, whereas such desires do not themselves have an authoritative aspect. To act in accord with our nature, Butler argued, is not necessarily to follow our strongest motive, but is rather to heed the authority of principles. Neither self-love nor benevolence, however, is the supremely authoritative principle in our nature. That office, he claimed, belongs instead to conscience.[4]

Conscience, for Butler, performs two separate tasks. First of all, it determines the proper scope of benevolence. Not in every case, Butler rightly observed, are we required to fix our attention on the general happiness and suspend the special concern we have only for those (e.g., family, friends) with whom we share particular interests (XII:3). Here conscience appeals to the principle of partiality and to what have been called "agent-centered prerogatives," permitting us to engage in long-term projects and hold by standing commitments whose value and very possibility a constant demand to maximize the general good would undermine.[5] The second task of conscience for Butler is to forbid the pursuit of the general welfare when it entails breaking certain sorts of obligations we bear toward others. The duties of fidelity, honor, and what he calls strict justice (e.g., not killing an innocent other to prevent a greater loss of life) we cannot justify upon the basis of benevolence. For all we know, an unjust man might procure himself an advantage far greater than the harm he did others, and yet we would not approve of his action; considerations of benevolence alone, Butler noted wisely, would easily excuse the most shocking cases of adultery (XII:31 [footnote]; DNV:8–10). So conscience appeals to "agent-centered restrictions," duties that are overriding even though their performance may seem not to be what would lead to the most general happiness. In short, conscience for Butler limits the demands of general benevolence, pointing out when we are morally permitted to pursue particularistic projects and when we are obliged to do what may not tally with our estimate of the general welfare. It implements, therefore, what I earlier called the principles of partiality and deontology, in order to limit the authority of general benevolence, which corresponds to what I called consequentialism. Butler offered no real "argument" for why, contrary to Hutcheson (his great utilitarian predecessor), benevolence cannot be the whole of virtue and conscience must give a separate (and higher) authority to deontological and particularistic duties – only an appeal to what we believe or should believe about particular cases. Yet it is unclear what more could be required. If the point of moral theory is to refine and guide our practice, settled moral convictions must always count for more than theoretical simplicity.

Now even if we believe that what he calls duties of strict justice must override considerations of the general happiness, we must have some sense of dissatisfaction or regret that benevolence should have to be set aside. In a fundamentally good world, we might believe, there would not be such moral costs. It is to these sentiments, which lie at the source of a great deal of theology, that Butler responded as did many religious thinkers before him. Not content with simply ranking these principles, he insisted that the divine administration, God's moral government of the world, will ensure that even when we must choose deontology over benevolence, the principle of benevolence will not go unsatisfied after all. God's end in giving us our nature was to bring about the general happiness, Butler maintained, and so our subordinating benevolence to deontology is precisely God's way of bringing that about, although we cannot grasp how that should be so.[6] Butler believed there is a similar divinely arranged convergence of partiality and general benevolence, although he discussed it far less. I shall focus upon his account of deontology and consequentialism.

In Butler's view, therefore, conflicts between these principles, although real enough for us, are only apparent *sub specie aeternitatis*. They stem from our relative ignorance. Had we God's perspective, we would see how the dictates of these principles coincide. From that perspective, though not from ours, it is not the case that by doing our duty our action may bring about more evil or less good than otherwise. Our limited ability to foresee consequences would, by itself, pose an obstacle to God's plan: Following benevolence on the basis of what we know would in many cases lead us astray. But Butler's God solves this problem by giving to finite intelligences a nature that assigns deontology authority over general benevolence.

Let us call "indirect consequentialism" the doctrine that whereas actions must be *justified* consequentially, they may have to be *motivated* by nonconsequentialist considerations.[7] Then Butler's God appears to be an indirect consequentialist. For the sake of promoting the general happiness, He has given us a nature for which benevolence is not always the supremely authoritative motive. Such a ranking of deontology over benevolence is what I shall call a *reconciliation ranking*: Setting A over B is the best way of pursuing A and of pursuing B (i.e., a better way of pursuing B than setting B first). A similar reconciliation ranking of deontology and benevolence, but without divine guarantees, has been proposed by many indirect utilitarians such as Sidgwick: "The doctrine that Universal Happiness is the ultimate *standard* must not be understood to imply that Universal Benevolence

136

is the only right or always best *motive* of action . . . it is not necessary that the end which gives the criterion of rightness should always be the end at which we consciously aim."[8]

But this brings us to the crux of the problem. Butler's reconciliation ranking depends on theological premises we can no longer accept, or at least not so assuredly as he did. But it has the merit of being an exercise in *theodicy*. That is, Butler recognized that from our perspective all is not right in the moral order of the universe: *Our* considered judgments about what is our duty can be at odds with what *we* can recognize to be the action leading to most happiness or good overall. And so he required that God as creator ensure that this disorder be only apparent. However, the secular utilitarian's assurances that such conflicts are only apparent will scarcely be as cogent as divine revelation. We can have no confidence any of us will be able to see things – in Sidgwick's phrase – "from the point of view of the universe." Theodicy may be impossible, but it is a response to what must remain for us a genuine problem. Without theodicy, reconciliation rankings carry no conviction; they are merely speculative. Here, as often elsewhere, secular ethics should refrain from mimicking theology.

Thus, the question arises of how we should handle conflicts between consequentialism and deontology, once we have dispensed with theological guarantees. We will not be able to cast aside our sense that we ought not to do certain things, even if thereby less good comes about in the world than otherwise. Although the only way to prevent ten being killed may be that we ourselves kill one of them (otherwise, for example, an extortioner will do away with all ten), we cannot help but believe that this is something we ought not to do. The killing of the ten is not our fault, we will say, but the extortioner's. Our hands must remain clean. Nonetheless, without the confidence that there is a God who will set things right in the end, we also cannot but hesitate whether holding to this absolute prohibition should remain so decisive a consideration. When the greater evil (which will ensue if we heed our deontological duty) is not too great, or where there lingers some uncertainty that it will indeed occur, we will no doubt abide by deontological constraints. But there comes a point when this may be a posture too difficult to maintain – not because of moral backsliding, but rather because the pull of other moral (consequentialist) reasons becomes too great. Without God, we may feel that we must assume more responsibility ourselves, not just for what we ourselves do, but for the way the world will go.

I do not think there is any systematic principle that will decide these conflicts. Of what form could such a principle be, consequentialist or deontological? That would seem circular. What counts as too great an evil or as overriding certainty? To some extent these are questions of judgment, if not of systematic principle. But there are limits to what φρόνησις can discern here. Sometimes rational persons will not agree about what decisions to make. *Hier scheiden sich die Geister.*

Thus, if we detach morality from religion, we must reckon with a fundamental *heterogeneity* of morality. By this I mean that we have an allegiance to several different moral principles that urge independent claims upon us (we cannot plausibly see the one as a means for promoting the other) and so can draw us in irreconcilable ways. The ultimate sources of moral value are not one, but many. This heterogeneity holds, whatever our situation. Under ordinary circumstances, we may continue to rank deontological above consequentialist reasons, but without Butler's confidence that the subordinate principle will be thereby best served: This is a ranking that does not reconcile, but sacrifices. Extraordinary circumstances – where we are certain that heeding the deontological claim would let a grave evil come about – can pull this structure apart. Because Butler saw so distinctly the variety of moral reasons that we acknowledge, and because he made so clear how religion alone can secure their unity, he commands our attention in a way that no other moral philosopher in the eighteenth century (not even Kant, as we shall see) can do. He set the terms of the debate between deontology and consequentialism for the succeeding centuries.[9]

PARTIALITY

I want now to look at these different principles of practical reason in some more systematic detail, beginning with the claims of partiality. To do this, however, I must first look more carefully at consequentialism. My earlier characterization of consequentialism – that we should do that action that will bring about the most good or the least evil overall – was necessarily vague. Just what is the good we should maximize? And if there is more than one sort of good, is the maximization of each sort equally urgent?

At the risk of gross simplification I shall distinguish four sorts of things that are called "good":

1. the avoidance of physical pain,
2. the satisfaction of needs,
3. whatever satisfies short-term preferences, and
4. whatever fulfills long-term preferences (projects and commitments).

I have not given "pleasure" as a category of the good because its contours are far less distinct than those of pain; I have distributed it among the other three categories. It should also be noted that while goods of category (2) are typically states of mind (e.g., pleasure), I am not requiring that those of categories (3) and (4) be so. On the contrary, what will satisfy our preference may well be something distinct from the state of mind it produces in us, as, for instance, the friendships we want differ from the pleasure that having them causes in us. By "needs" I shall mean desires that are ours not in virtue of our having adopted them, but rather in virtue of our being the sort of beings we all are (so desires for food and sleep, for example, would be needs). Preferences, by contrast, are desires we have because we have adopted them. Of course, we cannot acquire any desire simply at will: Preferences are those desires we acquire through or as a result of what we do voluntarily. I do not pretend that the boundary between preferences and needs must always be a sharp one. The intensity and specific character of a need is something over which we can have some control, and perhaps we also need that there be some of our preferences that do get satisfied. Furthermore, the distinction between short-term preferences and long-term projects is clearly one of degree, but this fact will not affect the points I shall make. Finally, if a person claims that something is good only for him or for some, then he is viewing it as a *subjective* good; but if he claims that it is good for everyone, that everyone has a reason to pursue it, then he is asserting that it is an *objective* good.[10]

Now the safest generalization to offer about the good is that people will largely differ about what is good (and what is better) with regard to short-term and long-term preferences. Desires we develop on our own are likely to diverge, and so what appears good in the light of them will be various. When persons view these preferences as being for something subjectively good, there will be just variety, but when they understand these preferences as being for something objectively good, there will then be disagreement. About the other forms of the good, however, there will be a far greater unanimity. First, we tend to agree about what causes physical pain and what are needs that everyone has; that is, X will agree with Y about what causes Y physical pain or about what Y's needs are. Furthermore, these are things that each of us generally agrees to be objectively good: So if I agree with Y that he has a certain need, then I and everyone else have a reason to pursue its satisfaction.

Only these two sorts of good have both the properties of unanimity and objectivity (preferences can be for what is believed to be objectively good, but they will not be widely shared). This explains, I believe, why they have an urgency that the other forms of good do not have – an urgency distinct from the subjective intensity with which they may be desired (we can imagine a preference held as strongly as a need, and yet it would not be as urgent).[11] Their urgency is responsible not only for the fact that they will count for more when we seek to do what will bring about the best overall, but also for the fact that their maximization is what gives consequentialism its force with respect to the other two practical principles.

To see this, let us turn now to conflicts between consequentialism and partiality. We would be unable to commit ourselves to particularistic projects, involving substantial ideals of the good life, if we believed that we should always do whatever is best overall for all concerned (unless that were indeed our project). Such commitments are valuable only if they steadfastly shape and orient what we do; their implementation cannot be provisional, revocable at a moment's notice, just because of what others happen to prefer or decide. Precisely this sort of flexibility, however, is what the principle of consequentialism requires. If we were only consequentialists, we constantly would have to set aside our own projects and friendships, since each of us has countless opportunities for increasing preference-satisfaction within a wider sphere. (The consequentialist riposte that firm friendships are indeed to be prized because, by focusing our efforts, they serve to advance the general good is merely speculative and, anyway, unlikely to please our friends; friendship depends on the shared belief that one cares more about one's friends than about others.[12])

Now to the extent that the greater good overall we could bring about has to do with others' preferences, we are within our rights to ignore the call of consequentialism. Saints, friends of humanity, and do-gooders are free to make that greater good their concern (this is, after all, their project), but not everyone need follow their example. When the greater good overall consists in the avoidance of pain or the satisfaction of needs, however, we cannot so easily pass over its claims upon us. If we have it in our power to satisfy the needs of others or to prevent their having physical pain, and if the good thereby effected is sufficiently great, we may well feel obligated to set aside temporarily the pursuit of our own projects. And even if we do not conclude that the greater good overall should prove decisive, we ought still to feel regret, or offer some explanation, or perhaps make some amends. I am disinclined to believe that there is any illuminating general rule to decide such cases (How great should the greater good overall be? How much does it matter how it is distributed among others?). Some cases may be decidable by judgment; others must be the object of rational disagreement. My aim is just to point out that consequentialist considerations have a strong claim to override the principle of partiality, only if the greater good overall is of specific sorts.

In this light the fundamental error of utilitarianism, in both its classical and more recent forms, appears to have been twofold. By failing to discriminate among different kinds of good, it has made the moral weight of desires depend simply upon the felt intensity with which they are held, and not upon their real urgency, and it has also made the maximum satisfaction of such indiscriminate desires the supreme value overall. Nonetheless, despite this simplification and over-generalization, consequentialist concerns cannot be dismissed as having no place at all in our moral deliberation.

How should we look at conflicts between partiality and deontology? Too little attention has been given, I believe, to the important way in which these conflicts differ from those between partiality and consequentialism. In fact, some philosophers apparently believe that deontological claims have no greater authority to override our particularistic commitments than do consequentialist claims.[13]

But this is not so. There are two reasons why consequentialist considerations need not prove superior in conflicts with our particularistic projects, and neither of these applies to deontological claims. First, bringing about the greatest good overall may certainly give way to such projects when the good involved is not of an urgent sort. Deontological claims, however, are always urgent. Because they issue absolute prohibitions, to the effect that we should never do certain kinds of actions, we cannot put them to one side *simply* on the grounds that our own projects direct us elsewhere. Sec-

142

ondly, consequentialist considerations, if unchecked, would threaten the very possibility of particularistic projects and commitments, since they would require that our actions be constantly at the disposal of everyone else's preferences and needs. By contrast, deontological claims set up a framework of what we may not do, a framework of side-constraints that generally far underdetermine the choices before us.[14] Only in exceptional cases will they require that we sacrifice the pursuit of our projects, so they are scarcely so inimical to personal commitments as consequentialism is. For all the urgency of its claims, deontology does not demand that we become moral fanatics in the way in which a consequentialism run wild would do. Consequentialist reasons alone cannot make room for the category of "the morally indifferent," whereas deontology can allow that there are other things in life besides morality.

It is, therefore, far more difficult to justify setting our own projects ahead of what we are deontologically required to do. Nonetheless, some deontological requirements are less decisive than others. Keeping a promise, for example, is a deontological duty: We have a reason to do it quite apart from whether it promotes the general good overall. (It may be true, as many consequentialists have speculated, that the shared practice of promise-keeping advances the general good; yet it remains hardly obvious that my breaking a promise will weaken this shared practice, and anyway this speculation, if true, gives us an *additional* reason for keeping our promises, and not the sole reason.) Nonetheless, we can easily imagine situations where some particularistic commitment – helping a friend or pursuing some crucial turn in our career – might properly prove more compelling than a promise. Kant believed that deontological duties must always override any empirically conditioned interest, because he thought that we must be committed to the ideal of autonomy, which distances us from such interests. But, as I argued earlier, the ideal of autonomy does not have the authority that Kant supposed. So universalistic morality (deontological as well as consequentialist, as we have seen before) need not always outweigh particularistic duties. Nonetheless, it is vastly more difficult to imagine a similarly proper decision where violating our deontological duty for the sake of some particularistic commitment would amount to physically harming or even killing another (who was innocent). Indeed, I am inclined to believe that such a decision is next to impermissible. If deontological prohibitions of the strictest sort may ever be overridden by a particularistic commitment, it could happen only in the case where failure to heed the principle of partiality would bring us to violate a similar deontological prohibition. Suppose, for example, your only two alternatives were to kill X or Y (both innocent), and X was your friend. Otherwise, such deontological claims must always prove more decisive.

THE ETHICS OF CONVICTION AND THE ETHICS OF RESPONSIBILITY

Toward the end of his famous essay *Politik als Beruf*, Max Weber distinguished between two moral outlooks – the ethics of conviction (*Gesinnungsethik*) and the ethics of responsibility (*Verantwortungsethik*). The ethics of conviction insists that our duty is to do certain things whether or not others put our actions to evil purposes: "The Christian does rightly and leaves the results with the Lord"; so it is an ethic in which deontological requirements reign supreme. The ethics of responsibility, by contrast, claims that it is irresponsible to settle on what one ought to do apart from what others are likely to do as a result. The fact that evil can come from good, and good from evil, is – for this outlook – not just a regrettable feature of the world, but the basis on which we should make our decisions; so this ethic is equivalent to consequentialism. These two ethics can collide even within a liberal-political order, since neither deontological nor urgent consequentialist duties rest upon disputable ideals of the good life. Weber believed that the politician, because his capacity is to represent the people as a whole, should act in accord with the ethics of responsibility. But this was not his last word. There can come a point, he added, where even in political office an individual may properly refuse to follow this ethic: Certain things he just cannot do, so that he will exclaim, "Here I stand, I can do no other." So Weber concluded that we must try to strike a balance between the two moral outlooks (if politics goes necessarily with an ethics of responsibility, then the politician must recognize that he is not just a politician).[15] Sometimes, however, such conflicts will prove rationally irresoluble.

I want now to look more carefully at conflicts between the principles of deontology and consequentialism. That there can indeed be conflicts in this area should be beyond dispute, for it cannot be plausible to deny any force whatsoever to one or the other of these principles. Such an extremist position (of a deontological sort) does seem to have been Kant's, at least in his essay "Über ein vermeintes Recht aus Menschenliebe zu lügen," where he disallowed any moral weight at all (whether or not decisive) to advancing the general good (in his example, preventing the murder of a friend) when that would require us to tell a lie.[16] Kant's error is not so much the decision he counseled, although that is bad enough, but rather his inability to recognize that this decision, even were it correct, brings with it a *moral loss* as well. In a crucial way, therefore, Kant was a far less perceptive moralist than Butler, or Weber, or Benjamin Constant, whom he was criticizing in that essay. He missed the radical heterogeneity of moral value.

One way to gain a firmer systematic grasp of such conflicts is to examine more closely the structure of deontological reasons. Thomas Nagel has written that deontological reasons differ from consequentialist ones in that they are *agent-relative*, as opposed to being *agent-neutral*. Something like Nagel's distinction between agent-relative and agent-neutral reasons can illuminate the difference between these two moral principles. But I am unhappy with the definition he gives of "agent-relativity": A reason is "agent-relative," he claims, if it includes an essential reference to the person to whom it applies. But this, I think, is too vague. Just as I have a (deontological) duty to give you the book if *I* promised to do so, so I have a (consequentialist) duty to relieve your pain if *I* am the one best able to do so. In both cases the reason why I have the duty makes essential reference to me, to some property I alone have.[17]

Nonetheless, the term "agent-relativity" can be used to pick out that distinctive feature of deontological reasons that Kant, Weber, and others have had in mind. Let us draw a distinction between the alternatives that *the agent alone* would be responsible for and the foreseeable consequences of these alternatives for which, however, *others* would be responsible. Then his deontological duties are those that he can recognize as his in looking solely at those alternatives for which he alone would be responsible. I can know that I have a duty to keep a promise without consulting what others will do as a result of my carrying it out. By contrast, I cannot know I have the (consequentialist) duty to satisfy someone's needs unless I have an idea of what others are likely to do as a result (of my doing or failing to do it), what needs they will acquire thereby. This explains why doing what is deontologically right can lead to there occurring a greater evil overall. Suppose, again, that if you do not kill one person, an extortioner will kill ten. Deontologically you should prefer killing none to killing one; consequentially the best overall would be that none be killed, the second best that one be killed, and the worst that ten be killed. Because of the situation, however, these two rankings point in altogether opposite directions: What is deontologically best will lead to what is consequentially worst. Yet that situation, the fact that your doing your duty will lead to great evil, is of the other's making. From a deontological perspective this fact is crucial. You by yourself are not responsible for it, and so it should play no role in your decision about what to do. This is the sense in which deontological reasons are "agent-relative": They are relative to what the agent alone – as opposed to others – is responsible for. Kant's universalizability test is clearly agent-relative in this way. We are to determine whether our maxim is morally permissible, he claimed, by looking at what would follow if everyone else *were* to act on it, and not by considering, as a consequentialist would, what will follow because of what everyone else *will* do (including immoral actions) as a result of our acting on it.

The distinction between what an agent alone is responsible for and what others do as a result of what he does offers, I think, a firmer basis for marking the difference between deontology and consequentialism than most of the usual definitions of these principles. For example, the view that consequentialism, unlike deontology, makes the moral worth of actions depend also upon the moral worth of their consequences wobbles because there is no absolute way of demarcating what is an action from what are its consequences (everything hinges on what description of the action we choose). The distinction that I have utilized, however, does not have this relativity. Another frequent way of distinguishing these two principles has been to say that deontology makes the good a function of the right, whereas consequentialism (also called *teleology*) makes the right a function of the good.[18] But this contrast also fails. The consequentialist duty of bringing about the most good overall is one whose goal is shaped by the principle that one ought to be impartial between one's own good and that of others.[19] So consequentialism, too, makes the good dependent on the right. For this reason, I believe it best to reserve the phrase "priority of the right over the good" for the usage that Kant gave it and that, as I showed in Chapter 4, is tied to the notion of categorical obligation. (This element of Kant's ethics is not identical to his exclusively deontological position, for consequentialist duties are categorical, too.) The way I have proposed for distinguishing deontology and consequentialism is much clearer than the usual definitions. It also preserves the general spirit and the specific examples in which these two principles have been contrasted.

Of course, how far an agent's responsibility ought to extend is the point of dispute between deontology and consequentialism. An ethics of responsibility demands that we must hold ourselves responsible, not just for what we alone do, but also (to the extent this is in our power) for the way the world goes. Without the confidence that there is a God who sustains the moral order of the world, we cannot easily decline such an extension of our responsibility. No doubt this broader responsibility will carry with it a fair share of mistakes; but there seems no one else better suited to the job.

It would be wrong, however, to ascribe to *self-indulgence* our reluctance to break deontological constraints for the sake of a greater good overall. Deontological duties are misunderstood if construed as duties to ourselves, to preserve our moral purity. Properly understood, they are duties to others, obligations that we never treat others in certain ways. Thus, neither an ethics of conviction nor an ethics of responsibility, when issuing directives contrary to those of the other, can be simply written off as an aberration of moral consciousness. These conflicts stem from the heterogeneity of morality itself.

I have already expressed skepticism about there being any neat principle for resolving these conflicts, as well as those involving the principle of partiality. Still, my discussion has come up with a few rules of thumb, which I shall list in closing:

1. Consequentialist reasons become urgent, and so can be at least seriously considered as overriding those of partiality and deontology, only when the greater good overall involves the avoidance of pain and the satisfaction of needs.

2. Deontological reasons of the strictest sort are always more decisive than those of partiality, except where failure to heed a particularistic consideration would amount to our violating a similar deontological claim.

3. Urgent consequentialist reasons *can* be reasonably held to be stronger than the strictest deontological ones, only when the greater evil that doing our deontological duty would lead to is significantly grave and significantly certain.

Judgment is clearly required by the first and third rules, but its power here is severely limited. Often there is no firm basis for judging in these cases what is overridingly urgent or significantly grave and certain, so little is to be gained from insisting that reasonable beings must be willing, under these circumstances, to put consequentialist reasons above particularistic ones or above the strictest deontological ones.

For this reason it might be argued that in conflicts between urgent consequentialist considerations and the strictest deontological ones, we should suspend judgment about in which of the two our obligation lies (even if we do have to choose to act on one of the alternatives). Suspension of judgment will be the right attitude to strike, I think, when we have some reason to believe that there may come further information that will alter our perception of the situation.[20] But not every conflict of this sort arises out of ignorance. Sometimes we are rightly confident that no new decisive facts are in the offing. We know that the conflict is irresolvable. Then, far from knowing too little, we know too much. We know that both the consequentially best and the deontologically best are our obligations and that we cannot carry out both. It is not that either is then permissible, but rather that both are obligatory. This means that in such cases we must surrender the axiom that "ought" implies "can" in the sense that connects obligation and feasibility. (Earlier in Chapter 4 I examined the different sense of " 'ought' implies 'can' " that links obligation and motivation.) But this axiom, too, has surely received too much uncritical approval anyway.[21] My reason for thinking this is what I take to be an important truth about our idea of morality, one which, despite their similarities noted at the beginning, draws moral reasoning away from scientific reasoning. Our deepest moral commitments – that we ought to abide by the strictest deontological requirements and that we ought to bring about the greatest urgent good overall – are commitments whose meaning for us (whatever their origin) is that we *come* with them *to* the world, and not that we *infer* them *from* the world. That is, their role is not even that of (scientific) "background knowledge," something we once learned, which guides our inquiries now, but which in principle remains subject to revision or rejection. Instead, these commitments are what make us moral agents at all.[22]

Recognizing this does not return us to a foundationalist moral epistemology. All justification remains contextual, since these fundamental moral commitments do not admit, I believe, of any justification at all. Nor are they "absolute presuppositions," except in the sense that we cannot understand what it would be to be moral agents and not to hold them fast. They set the limits of moral intelligibility.

So when we find that heeding both sorts of ultimate moral commitments is at odds with the way the world is, when we cannot do what they tell us we ought to do, we cannot entertain revising their authority or suspending judgment. We have to live with the fact that we have obligations we cannot honor. Our possibilities in the world are then too narrow for what we know we ought to do.

Conclusion

The fundamental aim of this book has been to show why moral philosophy must outgrow the simplifications that have beset its past. My intention, however, has not been to deny the possibilities or the importance of moral theory. I do not believe that the complexity of morality is so great, so boundless, that it baffles any attempt at systematization. I have argued, instead, that in three fundamental respects it eludes the simplistic notions of moral order with which moral philosophy, ancient and modern, has generally operated.

Let me summarize, once again, what these dimensions of moral complexity are. First, virtue cannot be understood simply as conscientious adherence to principle, because the moral rules associated with many of the virtues require the use of judgment if we are to know when and how we should exercise these virtues. Secondly, moral considerations having a decisive and overriding authority within the political realm do not have to have a similar priority outside that realm, in our "personal ideals." Thus, neutrality can be the paramount political value of the liberal state, without having to supplant in other areas of social life the constitutive attachments that we may have to some specific and controversial idea of the good life. Finally, instead of supposing that the structure of morality must be in the end either deontological or consequentialist, and instead of assuming that either all or none of our moral obligations are categorical, we should recognize that the ultimate sources of moral value are not one, but many.

I have tried to chart the structure of each of these forms of moral complexity. I have also said something (although surely not enough) about their interconnections. So my hope has not been that we should put the task of moral theory behind us, but rather that we should pursue it with less blinkered expectations. There is, however, one apparent exception to this – my account of moral judgment. At the end of Chapter 1 I suggested that although we can grasp in a general way what situations call for the exercise of judgment, what tasks it is to perform, and what are the preconditions of its acquisition, we seem unable to develop a theoretical understanding of how in fact moral judgment is exercised. Yet this thesis expresses a weaker curb on the ambitions of theory than may initially appear. Not only can we give a theoretical account of the circumstances and function of moral judgment, but we also have other forms of knowledge that let us recognize it when it exists. The exercise of moral judgment should not be thought a "mystery," just because it is not an object of theory. If, indeed, we could work out a broader notion of theory that would encompass more than merely the reconstruction of underlying rules, there would be no reason to hold that moral judgment eludes theoretical understanding. In any case, it should be clear that my treatment of the other two dimensions of moral complexity does not harbor any reservations about the scope of moral theory. There I appeal instead for a greater flexibility of theory.

I should conclude by observing, however, that here as elsewhere one's moral philosophy inevitably expresses the kind of person that one, if not is, then wants to be. The simplifications that I have attacked do not stem merely from a liking for theoretical simplicity. They also embody ideals of the moral person, and draw their force from these ideals. They manifest a drive to make virtue easily masterable (by reducing it to the conscientious adherence to principle), a wish to live life as a whole animated by a single dominant purpose, and a hope for an existence uncompromised by moral loss and unriven by unsettlable conflict. Thus, in arguing that certain simplified models of moral order do not agree with the phenomena, I have been claiming in effect that these moral ideals fail to square with our well-considered moral beliefs. Rejecting these ideals might be an occasion for some regret, if it were not that they deny so much of incalculable value.

Notes

PREFACE

1. In instances where it is unavoidable, the masculine pronoun has been used in the generic sense to mean "he or she."
2. A fine expression of this thought can be found somewhat later in Paine, *Rights of Man* (Part 2, Chapter 5): "I do not believe that any two men, on what are called doctrinal points, think alike who think at all. It is only those who have not thought that appear to agree." See also the recent essay by Luhmann, "The Improbability of Communication," 122–32.
3. See Hampshire, *Morality and Conflict*; Nagel, "The Limits of Objectivity," 77–139; and Williams, *Ethics and Philosophy*.
4. See the definitions of *Zweckrationalität* and *Wertrationalität* in Weber, *Wirtschaft und Gesellschaft*, 12–13.
5. See Chapter 2 of this book.

CHAPTER 1. MORAL JUDGMENT – AN ARISTOTELIAN INSIGHT

1. Kant, *Grundlegung zur Metaphysik der Sitten*, 408.
2. Kant, *Kritik der reinen Vernunft*, 1781 (= A), 134, and 1787 (= B), 174. See also the first two paragraphs of Kant's essay, "Über den Gemeinspruch," 201–3.
3. Kant, *Kritik der praktischen Vernunft*, 67–71.
4. Cf. Tugendhat, "Antike und moderne Ethik," in *Probleme der Ethik*, 35–56, especially 40ff.
5. The reason for this qualification appears at the end of the next section.

6. The extent to which moral judgment goes beyond the content of the schematic rules that it applies calls to mind what Ryle termed "knowing how," as opposed to "knowing that," except that Ryle does not seem to consider the possibility that "knowing how" may cite reasons without applying a rule that makes them reasons. See Ryle, *The Concept of Mind*, 25ff.

7. Moral conflict is best conceived not as the incompatibility of different moral duties in the abstract, but rather as the incompatibility of the actions they would require in a given situation. On this point, cf. Williams, *Problems of the Self*, 166f.

8. Cf. Nagel, "The Fragmentation of Value," in *Mortal Questions*, 128f.

9. Prichard, "Does Moral Philosophy Rest on a Mistake?" in *Moral Obligation*, 1–17; the quotation is from p. 11.

10. Aristotle, *Nicomachean Ethics*, 1128b33f. and 1105a30ff. In contrasting the ethics of duty and the ethics of virtue, Prichard may also have been groping toward the distinction between right-based and good-based ethics; on the latter see "Kantian liberalism" in Chapter 4 of this book.

11. Cf. MacIntyre, *After Virtue*, 141, 216; and Dent, *Moral Psychology of Virtues*, 29ff.

12. Kant, *Die Metaphysik der Sitten*, Part 2 (Tugendlehre), 20f.

13. Ibid., 55–6.

14. Ibid., 56.

15. The *Critique of Judgment* does not deal with moral judgment; moreover, the general form of judgment with which it is chiefly concerned is "reflective" judgment rather than "determinant" judgment, which as the application of general rules to particular circumstances, covers what I have here been discussing as moral judgment.

16. I have tried to show not that judgment must remain a feature of our moral experience, but only that it pervades morality as we continue to understand it in large harmony with the past. Philosophy that has abjured the dubious charms of the a priori or of "conceptual analysis" can attempt no more. Notice, however, that judgment in the narrow sense presented in the First Critique will not disappear even if all moral rules cease to be schematic and unanimity is achieved about what "the moral perspective" consists in.

17. Aristotle, *Nicomachean Ethics*, 1104a9; see also *Eudemian Ethics*, 1217b33.

18. Aristotle, *Nicomachean Ethics*, 1179b30f.
19. Ibid., 1106b36.
20. Ibid., Book 2, Chapter 9.
21. For Aristotle's theory of the practical syllogism, see also *Nicomachean Ethics*, 1147a25f.
22. Ibid., 1109b23.
23. See Guicciardini's (1483–1540) criticism of Machiavelli's "science" of politics in *Ricordi*, §6: "É grande errore parlare delle cose del mondo indistintamente e assolutamente e, per dire cosí, per regola; perché quasi tutte hanno distinzione e eccezione per la varietà delle circunstanze, le quali non si possono fermare con una medesima mesura: e queste distinzione e eccezione non si truovano scritte in su libri, ma bisogna le insegni la discrezione."
24. Smith, *The Theory of Moral Sentiments*, Part 7, Section 4, 517; also Part 3, Chapter 6, 287f.
25. This is also fairly clear from a passage in Part 3, Chapter 6 (ibid., 284–93).
26. At the end of Part 6, Chapter 1 (ibid., 370–1), when denying that there is any absolute ordering of possibly conflicting obligations, Smith also correlated the function of moral judgment in adjudicating such conflicts with the sentiments of the supposed impartial spectator.
27. Gadamer, *Wahrheit und Methode*, 295ff.
28. However influential this technical image of natural science has been since the seventeenth century, it is importantly incorrect. See, for example, Kuhn's recent account of how the sciences require examples for just the reasons that I have associated with the role of judgment – the application of general principles to concrete cases: Kuhn, *The Essential Tension*, 293f.
29. Gadamer, "Über die Möglichkeit einer philosophischen Ethik," in *Kleine Schriften*, 179f.
30. Gadamer, *Wahrheit und Methode*, 290ff., 448.
31. Gadamer, "Rhetorik, Hermeneutik und Ideologiekritik," 57ff.
32. As Plutarch (*De Virtute Morali*, 443F) remarked, "φρόνησις τύχης δεῖται," judgment has need of chance.
33. The claim that the nature of moral judgment resists theoretical understanding does not imply that moral reasoning differs essentially from scientific reasoning. See Note 28.

CHAPTER 2. THE LIMITS OF ARISTOTELIANISM

1. MacIntyre, *After Virtue*, viii, 147, 182.
2. Ibid., 5off., 112. Not here, but elsewhere (p. 141) he recognizes that for Aristotle the exercise of the virtues comes to more than the observance of rules, because of the need for judgment. But this emendation does not affect materially the argument discussed here.
3. Ibid., 6ff., 56, 68.
4. Ibid., 30, 56ff., 182.
5. Ibid., 68. For a more positive evaluation of the link between individual freedom and bureaucracy, see the first section of Chapter 3 of this book.
6. Cf. Strauss, *Natural Right and History*, 5–8 (MacIntyre's most significant departure from Strauss's views is that despite his castigations of modernity, MacIntyre has a greater appreciation of moral conflict and a larger openness to pluralism; see Note 32.); Arendt, *The Origins of Totalitarianism*, 299; Adorno and Horkheimer, "Excursus II: Juliette or Enlightenment and Morality," in *Dialectic of Enlightenment*, 81–119.
7. One important example of such gross simplification is that MacIntyre takes Aristotelianism as the representative morality of antiquity. However, the polis, which formed the framework for many of its distinctive features that MacIntyre prizes, was a historically limited and relatively marginal social form even in antiquity. A far greater part of the history of ancient society (even before the triumph of Christianity) took place under the quite different conditions of empire. Largely because of this, Stoicism played no less important a role among the educated classes than Aristotelianism did. And Stoic moral thought anticipates much of what MacIntyre believes to be essential to modernity (e.g., role-distance). See, for example, Seneca, *Epistulae Morales* V, in *Letters from a Stoic*, 37: "Imagine what the reaction would be if we started dissociating ourselves from the conventions of society. Inwardly everything should be different but an outward face should conform with the crowd." Indeed, MacIntyre himself recognizes the similarities between Stoicism and what he rejects in modernity (MacIntyre, op. cit., 131, 157f.). A more sober view, therefore,

would be that role-distance is no more peculiar to modernity than to antiquity. And in any case it is not an essentially universal feature of modern life (see Chapter 5 of this book).

8. MacIntyre, op. cit., 35–59.

9. Ibid., 65, 67.

10. Ibid., 60f., 62, 240.

11. Ibid., 17, 66.

12. Ibid., 51.

13. Ibid., 56–7.

14. I cannot here develop this contextualist theory of justification in all the detail that it requires. But two remarks are necessary to avoid misunderstandings: (1) Such a theory does not claim that beliefs are justified just because they are held and not disputed. Beliefs, simply as beliefs that are held, are not objects of justification, because (2) only when the question arises whether to add or to reject a belief does that belief become an object of justification. We might say that for contextualism, questions of justification fix only on *changes* in beliefs. This is the view of epistemology that we find, for example, in C. S. Peirce.

15. For some limits to the analogy between science and morality, see the end of Chapter 6 of this book.

16. This is perhaps why elsewhere MacIntyre treats Kant's and Reid's ethics as a "secularization of Protestant Christianity." See MacIntyre's essay, "How Moral Agents Became Ghosts," 305ff.

17. Cf. Butler, *Analogy of Religion and Sermons*, sermons 2 (paragraph 8) and 3 (paragraph 3); Rousseau, *Du Contrat Social*, Book 1, Chapter 8; Kant, *Grundlegung zur Metaphysik der Sitten*, Chapter 3. On this similarity between Rousseau and Kant, see the two monographs by Cassirer, *Rousseau, Kant, Goethe* and *The Question of Jean-Jacques Rousseau*.

18. That is, the autonomy of morality is not the same as Kant's notion of the autonomy of the moral agent, which I discuss in Chapters 4 and 5.

19. Aristotle, *Nicomachean Ethics*, 1097b1f. The following interpretation of this passage resembles that given by Ackrill, "Aristotle on *Eudaimonia*," 15–33. Pleasure and external goods Aristotle also considered as elements of the fulfilled life, but only to the extent that they are, respectively, a supervenient quality or a precondition for the exercise of virtue. See Aris-

totle, *Nicomachean Ethics*, Book 1, Chapter 8. My general view that for Aristotle morality is an autonomous source of value is quite close to the position developed by McDowell in "The Role of Eudaimonia in Aristotle's Ethics," 359–76.

20. On this point see Finnis, *Natural Law and Natural Rights*, 33f., 52f.

21. MacIntyre, *After Virtue*, 139–40, 172.

22. Aristotle, *Nicomachean Ethics*, Book 10, Chapter 7. Aristotle even asserts that in contemplation we attain our "true self" ("εκαστοσ ε'ιναι). Although for him there are material and social preconditions for becoming our true selves, what we then are puts us beyond society. Cf. ibid., 1166a 15–24, 1168b 30–5, 1178a 1–5.

23. For Aristotle's view that morality flourishes best in political activity, see his *Nicomachean Ethics*, Book 1, Chapter 2, and also 1103b 2–7, 1177b 6f., 1180a 29f.; *Eudemian Ethics* 1215b 1–5; and *Politics*, Book 3, Chapter 9. For obvious reasons this view does not reappear in a medieval Aristotelian such as Aquinas, who claimed only that the state should aim at fostering solely those virtues ordainable to the common good (Aquinas, *Summa Theologica* I–II Q.XCVI, a.3) and that the common good of the state cannot flourish unless those citizens who govern are virtuous (ibid. Q.XCII, a.1, reply Obj.3). So Aquinas clearly recognized that some moral virtues are best exercised outside of the political realm, an idea that jars with his continued appeal to the Aristotelian idea that "man is a *part* of the state" (loc. cit.).

24. Kant's idea of the summum bonum includes the claim that forms of self-fulfillment must always be subordinated to the dictates of universalistic morality. For doubts about this see Chapters 4 and 6 of this book.

25. MacIntyre, *After Virtue*, 152, 183, 169–209. I suggested earlier that the dependence of Aristotle's ethical thought upon a "metaphysical biology" has been overestimated. We shall see that MacIntyre's view of the good life differs from Aristotle's, not in its metaphysical economy but in other respects.

26. Ibid., 175, 181.

27. Ibid., 183, 187f., 190ff.

28. Ibid., 204. See also the similar criticism in Schneewind, "Virtue, Narrative, and Community," 653–63.

29. I am unaware of any passage where Aristotle explicitly rules

out the possibility of moral conflict (although the pseudo-Aristotelian *Magna Moralia* 1200a5 does do so), but he does argue that the virtues cannot exist independently of one another in any individual (*Nicomachean Ethics*, Book 6, Chapter 13). This passage was used by later Aristotelians, such as Aquinas, to formulate the doctrine of the unity of the virtues, which certainly did work to rule out moral conflict: According to Aquinas one cannot act courageously if one is not at the same time acting in accord with the other virtues. See Acquinas, *Summa Theologica* I–II, Q.LXV, a.1.

30. MacIntyre, *After Virtue*, 134, 148, 153, 167.
31. Ibid., 134, 208.
32. See my discussion of Weber in Chapter 6. For Leo Strauss, too, Weber's position is morally bankrupt, but not so much because of any general subjectivism about morals as because of Weber's belief that there are irresolvable moral conflicts (Strauss, *Natural Right and History*, 36ff., 64ff.). So Strauss shows a better perception of Weber's thought, although MacIntyre's is the more mature moral position. For Berlin's position, see his *Four Essays on Liberty*, Lff., 167ff.; and also Williams's introduction to Berlin, *Concepts and Categories*.
33. MacIntyre, *After Virtue*, 236.
34. I shall return to the criticism of this terminology in Chapter 5.

CHAPTER 3. LIBERALISM AND THE NEUTRALITY OF THE STATE

1. Aristotle, *Nicomachean Ethics*, Book 1, Chapter 3.
2. Cf. Weber, *Wirtschaft und Gesellschaft*, 198, 505, 826.
3. Oakeshott, *Rationalism in Politics and Other Essays*, 1–36.
4. It should be clear that my sympathies lie more with the jurisprudential, than with the civic humanist (neo-Aristotelian) tradition of modern political thought. On this distinction see Pocock, *Virtue, Commerce, and History*, 37–50.
5. This is the point ignored in Brian Barry's argument that political neutrality is impossible. See his *Political Argument*, 75–9.
6. See the brilliant discussion of this joint increase of state power

and individual rights in Durkheim, *Leçons de Sociologie*, 91–9.

7. Cf. Berlin, "Two Concepts of Liberty," in *Four Essays on Liberty*, 118–62; and as typical of subsequent criticism, C. Taylor, "What's Wrong with Negative Liberty," in *Philosophical Papers*, vol. 2, 211–29.

8. The best discussions of the political significance of the public are Arendt, *The Human Condition*, and Habermas, *Strukturwandel der Öffentlichkeit*.

9. Sidgwick, *The Methods of Ethics*, 395ff.

10. Cf. Ackerman, *Social Justice in the Liberal State*, 11ff. Ackerman's fourth and remaining argument is that even if one thinks one knows what the good life is and that it is of a kind that can be forced on others, one cannot be sure that the right people will be doing the forcing. This seems to me rather weak. Often one could be sure of that, and even if there was some doubt, one might reasonably be willing to take the risk; furthermore, laws and regulations could be instituted to lessen the likelihood of abuse of power.

11. Ibid., 196. Ackerman seems aware of this fact, since he has more recently argued that "it would be a categorical mistake to imagine that there could be a Neutral justification for the practice of Neutral justification." (Idem, "What is Neutral about Neutrality?," 387.) With this I disagree.

12. I have sought to formulate only the most plausible part of Habermas's position (he also claims, implausibly, that the commitment to the ideal speech situation lies simply in language use itself). For the notion of an ideal speech situation, see Habermas, *Communication and the Evolution of Society*, 1–68; and idem, "Vorlesungen zu einer sprachtheoretischen Grundlegung," in *Vorstudien und Ergänzungen*, especially 104–26.

13. For the consensus theory of truth, see Habermas, "Wahrheitstheorien," in *Vorstudien und Ergänzungen*, 127–83.

14. See, for example, Habermas and Luhmann, *Theorie der Gesellschaft oder Sozialtechnologie*, 115; Habermas, *Vorstudien und Ergänzungen*, 122–3, 130f.; and idem, *Theorie und Praxis*, 25.

15. For example, see Lukes, "Of Gods and Demons," 139f.; and Geuss, *The Idea of a Critical Theory*, 66f.

16. Cf. Habermas, *Theorie des kommunikativen Handelns*, vol. 2, 586f.: "Only under the situational pressure of a problem which

confronts us are relevant parts of such a background consensus freed from the mode of unquestioned familiarity and brought to consciousness as something needing confirmation. ... Even in such situations only a small segment of background knowledge becomes uncertain, removed from inclusion in complex traditions, relations of solidarity, and competences. When an objective occasion arises for coming to agreement about a problematic situation, background knowledge is transformed into explicit knowledge only in a step-by-step fashion." See also Habermas, "Reply to my Critics," 255.

17. In "Liberalism," 113–43, Dworkin also connects the idea of neutrality with that of equal respect, although without any argument *why* "the government does not treat them [citizens] as equals if it prefers one conception of the good life to another" (p. 127). That is what my neutral justification of political neutrality tries to explain.

18. For his distinction, see Dworkin, *Taking Rights Seriously*, 180, 272f.

19. Cf. Hume, *An Inquiry Concerning Morals*, Section 5 (Part 2), footnote 8 and Section 9 (Part 1); and Hume, *Treatise of Human Nature*, 582f.

20. See the discussion of the connection between sympathy theories and utilitarianism in Rawls, *A Theory of Justice*, 183–92.

21. The relation between these two notions of respect has received far less attention than it deserves. For discussions of the distinction itself that are similar, though not identical, to mine, see Darwall, "Two Kinds of Respect," 36–49; and Tugendhat, *Probleme der Ethik*, 135ff.

22. On the connection between respect for persons and equal respect, see Williams, *Problems of the Self*, 234ff.

CHAPTER 4. THE POLITICAL ORDER AND PERSONAL IDEALS

1. Kant, *Kritik der praktischen Vernunft*, Analytic, Chapter 2.
2. Hume, *Treatise of Human Nature*, Book 3, Part 2, Section 1.
3. Cf. ibid., Section 2; and Hume, *An Inquiry*, Section 3 (Part 1).

The term "circumstances of justice" comes from Rawls, *A Theory of Justice*, 126ff. See also Warnock, *The Object of Morality*, Chapter 2.

4. Cf. Kant, *Die Metaphysik der Sitten*, Rechtslehre, §44. At one point Hume does come to recognize this point (*Treatise of Human Nature*, 555); but generally in the *Treatise* he assumes that conceptions of universal benevolence will coincide. See also Madison's 10th Federalist letter.

5. Reflexion 610 in the Akademie-Ausgabe of Kant's works, reprinted in Bittner and Cramer, *Materialien zu Kants Kritik*, 68.

6. Kant's reasoning here involves his ideal of autonomy, which I shall discuss later. It is best presented in his essay "Über den Gemeinspruch," Section 2, 235f., 252. See also Kant, *Die Metaphysik der Sitten*, Einleitung in die Metaphysik der Sitten, II; Rechtslehre, §44.

7. See Walzer, "Liberalism and the Art of Separation," 315–30.

8. Bodin, *Les Six Livres de la République*; Locke, *A Letter Concerning Toleration*; Bayle, *Commentaire philosophique*.

9. In this account of the difference between a right-based and a good-based ethics I am following closely the illuminating Chapter I.9 in Sidgwick's *Methods of Ethics*; the extent to which Plato and Aristotle made an attractive notion of the good fundamental would explain the difficulty in finding the idea of categorical obligation in their writings. Observe that on the line of thought I have adopted, the right is prior to the good, not only in "deontological," but also in "consequentialist" duties (see the Preface of this book), since these, too, are categorical. Thus, Kant's priority of the right over the good should not be confused with his additional doctrine that "deontological" duties must rank above "consequentialist" ones. In Chapter 6 I shall discuss more thoroughly the distinction between deontology and consequentialism, and explain why the usual equation between deontology and priority of the right will not work. (Pistorius's brilliant review is reprinted in Bittner and Cramer, op. cit., 144–60.).

10. It has been suggested that we restrict the term "morality" to universalistic duties and use the term "ethics" to cover both "morality" and particularistic duties (Williams, *Ethics and the Limits of Philosophy*. Although some facts of usage and intellectual history favor this terminology, I shall not follow it.

Nor shall I forego using the terms "duty" and "obligation" for whatever it is we ought morally (in the broad sense) to do. Some may find the phrase "duties and obligations of friendship" repellent, but I think that is because they associate "duty" and "obligation" with what one is disinclined to do or with what one is categorically bound to do, or with both. A more serious reason for limiting the sense of duty is that sometimes what one ought morally to do (e.g., show gratitude to a benefactor) does not imply corresponding rights in others (cf. Williams, op. cit., 179). But I shall not be assuming that "duties" and "obligations" must always entail corresponding rights in others. (Traditionally a distinction was made between perfect duties, which imply corresponding rights, and imperfect duties, which do not. See, for example, Mill, *Utilitarianism*, Chapter 5.)

11. For the idea that categoricity of duty implies nonempirical freedom, see Kant, *Kritik der praktischen Vernunft*, 19ff., 29.
12. Ibid., 4.
13. Ibid., 15, 41f.
14. Ibid., 97f.
15. Ibid., 87, 118. (The translation is Beck's, in Kant, *Critique of Practical Reason*, 122.)
16. On these two aspects of Kant's idea of freedom, see Beck, *Commentary on Kant's Critique*, 177ff.
17. Fichte, *Beitrag zur Berechtigung der Urtheile des Publikums über die französische Revolution*, in *Schriften zur Revolution*, 122, 125. Fichte's later organistic and nationalistic theory of the state is, of course, a different matter.
18. "Happiness contains everything (and nothing else but that) which nature can provide us, but virtue is that which only man himself can give or take away from himself." (Kant, Über den Gemeinspruch," 221.)
19. Kant's clearest expression of this argument is in Sections 1 and 2 of "Über den Gemeinspruch."
20. Kant, *Grundlegung zur Metaphysik der Sitten*, 433. I have said that Kant's ideal of the person corresponds to his ideal of political neutrality because of the shared detachment toward substantial notions of the good life. But this does not mean that there are not also important differences between these Kantian ideals: (1) Political neutrality forbids the state, but personal autonomy does not forbid individuals, from pur-

suing some substantial conception of the good life. (2) Political duties are *Rechtspflichten*, requiring only that we do not act to infringe the equal liberty of others, and so they can be the object of political coercion; but our autonomy is a *Tugendpflicht*, a matter of our inward disposition, and so it cannot be the object of political coercion.

21. Cf. Kant, *Kritik der praktischen Vernunft*, 22. This psychology, and the inordinate suspicion that it encourages about acknowledged motives and that recurs throughout the *Kritik* and the *Grundlegung*, is absent from Kant's earlier *Lectures on Ethics* of the period 1775–80. These lectures are, indeed, superior in almost every respect to his later ethics, as we shall see.

22. For explicit references, see Kant, *Kritik der praktischen Vernunft*, 36, 143 (footnote), 159; idem, *Kritik der reinen Vernunft*, B835. Cf. also Fichte's quip, "Der Mensch *kann*, was er *soll*; and wenn er sagt: ich *kann* nicht, so *will* er nicht" (Fichte, op. cit., 109).

23. Aristotle, *Nicomachean Ethics*, Book 3, Chapter 5; idem, *Eudemian Ethics*, Book 2, Chapters 7–9.

24. Aristotle, *Nicomachean Ethics*, Book 2, Chapters 1 and 3, and 1113b30–1114a30; also idem, *Eudemian Ethics*, 1225b14–16.

25. For the constitutive role of moral luck, see Williams, *Problems of the Self*, 207–29; idem, *Moral Luck*, 20–39; *Ethics and the Limits of Philosophy*, 174ff., and passim. Signs that on this matter he does not distinguish cleanly between scope and motivational basis occur in *Ethics and the Limits of Philosophy*, 189, 194, as well as in "Internal and External Reasons," *Moral Luck*, 101–113. Thus, if an "external" reason for A to do X is, as Williams defines it, a reason that need not be expressed in any of A's present motives nor be attainable by deliberation from those motives, then we should not say, as Williams does, that there can be no external reasons. Categorical obligations have just this sort of scope, and we may come to appreciate them, not by deliberation, but by training. On this point see MacIntyre's review of *Moral Luck*, "The Magic in the Pronoun 'My' ", 113–25.

26. Kant, *Lectures on Ethics*, 66. For the distinction between scope and motivational basis, see ibid., 36, 40; for the need for habituation, see ibid., 46, 56, 64. There is a similar picture in Butler, *Analogy of Religion*, 154f; and it seems to be the view

at which, in the end, Foot has arrived in *Virtues and Vices*, 157–73.

27. Cf. Kant, *Kritik der praktischen Vernunft*, 99f.
28. See O. W. Holmes, *The Common Law*, Lecture 2.
29. This confusion runs through Nagel, *The Possibility of Altruism*, 7, where "internalism" is successively defined as the position that "the presence of a motivation for acting morally is guaranteed by the truth of ethical propositions themselves," which I deny, and then as "the conviction that one cannot accept or assert sincerely any ethical proposition without accepting at least a prima facie motivation for action in accordance with it," which I do not deny. Because the whole debate about "internalism" and "externalism" is too often caught in this confusion, I have decided not to use these terms. For an earlier survey of the debate, see Frankena, "Obligation and Motivation in Philosophy," 40–81.
30. Cf. from Aristotle, *Nicomachean Ethics*, 1147b15 with 1144b26 and 1151a17.
31. My argument implies, in addition, that we need not share Kant's belief that universalistic morality (of the deontological sort) must always override particularistic morality. For more on this, see Chapter 6.

CHAPTER 5. POLITICAL ROMANTICISM

1. Herder, *Abhandlung über den Ursprung der Sprache*, II.ii; idem, *Ideen zur Philosphie der Geschichte der Menschheit*, IV.3, VIII.4, IX.4. The connection between instinctual poverty and the social character of the self appears often in Enlightenment writers, particularly in Montesquieu, to whom Herder was so indebted (cf. Montesquieu, *Oeuvres Complètes*, vol. 2, 230).
2. Herder, *Briefe zu Beförderung der Humanität* (1795), Sechste Sammlung, Sections 73 and 79.
3. Cf. Herder, *Auch eine Philosphie der Geschichte*, 46, 94, 102–6, 115. Again, this was not a thought unknown to the British and French Enlightenment. Cf. Gay, *The Enlightenment*, vol. 2, 104, 123.
4. Herder, *Ideen zur Philosphie*, VIII.5. "The notion of belonging,"

writes Berlin (*Vico and Herder*, 195), "is at the heart of all Herder's ideas."

5. Herder, *Auch eine Philosophie der Geschichte*, 46. In his later writings (the *Ideen* and the *Briefe*) Herder appealed to a general ideal of "Humanität," but without, I believe, thereby surrendering the principle that gains are inseparable from losses. The definition of this ideal (*Briefe*, Dritte Sammlung (1794), Section 27) speaks of "a feeling of human nature in its strength and weakness, in its deficiencies and perfections."

6. Cf. Herder *Ideen*, IX.1; idem, *Briefe* (1793), Erste Sammlung, Sections 14–16; idem, *Anhang zu den Briefen*, Section 11 (in *Sämtliche Werke*, vol. 18, 308–10.)

7. Herder, *Ideen*, IX.4. For his anarchism, see ibid., VIII.5; and for his praise of the polis, ibid., XIII.4.

8. This ambivalence of extremes is a recurrent feature of anti-liberal expressivism. See Note 37 below.

9. Schiller, *Über Anmut und Würde*, in *Schriften zur Philosphie und Kunst*, 44–50. Kant's reply appeared in *Die Religion innerhalb der Grenzen*, "Zusatz zum ersten Stück." Herder took over Schiller's critique, *Briefe*, Sechste Sammlung (1795), Section 73.

10. Cf. Schiller, *Über die ästhetische Erziehung des Menschen*, vierter Brief; and also letzter Brief: "der ästhetische Staat allein kann sie [die Gesellschaft] wirklich machen, weil er den Willen des Ganzen durch die Natur des Individuums vollzieht."

11. Novalis, *Glauben und Liebe* (1798), §19 in *Werke*, vol. 2, 295; Müller, *Elemente der Staatskunst*, vol. 1, 62, and vol. 2, 85. Similarly organic notions of state and society figured among Restoration apologists such as Bonald and de Maistre. The Romantics around Friedrich Schlegel differed from the French Reactionaries at first by the ironizing distance they cultivated toward the organic forms into which they wished to be absorbed (cf. Schlegel's *Athenäumsfragmente* of 1798). This irony faded with time, and the only remaining difference was their considerably greater political naivete. Cf. Reiss, *Political Thought of the German Romantics*. For an excellent survey of the Romantic infatuation with the organic, see Schlanger, *Les Métaphores de l'organisme*.

12. This is clear from the example of Benjamin Constant. Cf. S. T. Holmes, *Benjamin Constant*, 156–80.

13. Novalis, *Vermischte Bemerkungen* (1797–98), §115: "Es sind viele

antirevolutionäre Bücher für die Revolution geschrieben worden. Burkehat aber ein revolutionäres Buch gegen die Revolution geschrieben." (In *Werke*, vol. 2, 278.)

14. Charles Taylor seems to believe that these two ideas of autonomy and expressivism are reconciled in the Hegelian synthesis. Cf. his *Hegel*, 44. His interpretation underplays, however, the extent to which Hegel rejected the ideal of autonomy: Social institutions must be rationally transparent so that *Geist* will be self-subsistent and autonomous, Hegel thought, but individuals are to this *Geist* as accidents are to a substance. Cf. Hegel, *Grundlinien der Philosophie des Rechts* (hereafter *Rechtsphilosophie*), Section 145; and also his *Reason in History*, 52.

15. Hegel, *Theologische Jugendschriften*, 266f., 293–6. For an acknowledgment of Schiller's influence, see his letter to Schelling of 16 April 1795 (in Hegel, *Briefe*, vol. 1, 25).

16. Hegel, *Natural law*, 75ff., 112. Cf. also *Rechtsphilosophie*, Section 135. For an excellent analysis of the essay on natural law, see Hyppolite, *Introduction à la philosophie de Hegel*, Chapter 4.

17. Cf. Kant's notorious definition of marriage as "the union of two persons of the opposite sex for the lifelong, mutual possession of each other's sexual characteristics" (*Metaphysik der Sitten*, Rechtslehre, §24, 107), and Hegel's angry denunciation of it in *Rechtsphilosophie*, Section 75.

18. Hegel, *Rechtsphilosophie*, Section 147. For Hegel's account of *Sittlichkeit*, see ibid., Sections 142–56, as well as his *Reason in History*, 137f., and *Phänomenologie des Geistes*, V.B.1 and VI.A.

19. For Hegel's analysis of *Moralität*, see *Rechtsphilosophie*, Sections 105–14. For the idea that the classical Greeks had only *Gewohnheiten*, and not *Gewissen*, see idem, *Vorlesungen über die Philosophie der Geschichte*, 309, 323; also *Vorlesungen über die Geschichte der Philosophie*, vol. 2, 114; and *Enzyklopädie der philosophischen Wissenschaften*, Section 482. For a fine discussion of Hegel's effort to synthesize *Moralität* and *Sittlichkeit*, see Ritter, *Metaphysik und Politik*, 281–309.

20. See Hegel, *Enzyklopädie*, Section 516, and idem, *Rechtsphilosophie*, Section 150. See also the parallel chain of thought in Bradley's "My Station and Its Duties" (1876) in *Ethical Studies*, 98–147.

21. Cf. Hegel, *Differenz des Fichte'schen und Schelling'schen Systems*

der Philosophie (1801), pp. in *Jenaer Schriften*, 20ff. For Hegel's use of the organic/fragmented (or "atomistic") dichotomy in a political context, see his *Rechtsphilosophie*, Sections 156 (Zusatz), 255, 269 (Zusatz). The identity/difference, alienation/ reconciliation dichotomies occur, of course, throughout his writings. Avineri's *Hegel's Theory of the Modern State* and Plant's *Hegel* are very useful for tracing Hegel's continuing fascination with these dichotomies.

22. See Hegel, *Rechtsphilosophie*, Sections 75, 100, 258, for Hegel's critique of contractarianism.

23. Cf. Hegel, *Natural Law*, 113; idem, *System der Sittlichkeit* (1802/ 03), in *Schriften zur Politik und Rechtsphilosophie*, 460–3; idem, *Rechtsphilosophie*, Sections 3, 257ff.; and idem, *Reason in History*, 49ff. In *Hegel's Retreat from Eleusis*, 136ff., Kelly invokes the "neutrality" of the Hegelian state, but only his strange use of this term divides us. For Kelly it means, among other things, that this state "guarantees objectified truth to common life" and is founded upon law (*Recht*), Hegel's comprehension of which, he admits, "goes beyond the scope of civil law to include the entire content of morality, social ethics, and world history, all of what we may call 'practical reason.' "

24. Throughout his political writings Benjamin Constant, Hegel's contemporary, analyzed the totalitarian potential of efforts to make modern societies conform to the ideal of the polis. See above all his famous essay, "De la Liberté ancienne comparée à celle des modernes" (1819), recently reprinted with other relevant texts in Constant, *De la Liberté chez les Modernes*, 491– 515. For Hegel's diagnosis of the Reign of Terror as applied Kantianism, see his *Phänomenologie des Geistes*, VI. B. III ("Die absolute Freiheit und der Schrecken"), and *Rechtsphilosophie*, Section 29.

25. Note the progression of thought in the following passage from Hegel, *Rechtsphilosophie*, Section 260 (Zusatz): "Das Wesen des neuen Staates ist, dass das Allgemeine verbunden sei mit der vollen Freiheit der Besonderheit und dem Wohlergehen der Individuen, dass also das Interesse der Familie und bürgerlichen Gesellschaft sich zum Staate zusammennehmen muss, dass aber die Allgemeinheit des Zwecks nicht ohne das eigene Wissen und Wollen der Besonderheit, die ihr Recht behalten muss, fortschreiten kann. Das Allgemeine muss also betätigt sein, aber die Sub-

jektivität auf der anderen Seite ganz und lebendig entwick-
elt werden. Nur dadurch, dass beide Momente in ihrer
Stärke bestehen, ist der Staat als ein gegliederter und wahr-
haft organisierter anzusehen."

26.   Ibid., Section 272. Not surprisingly, therefore, Hegel de-
      nied the elementary liberal right of the individual to leave
      the state, except at the state's own desire; see ibid., Section
      75 (Zusatz).

27.   Cf. Haym, *Hegel und seine Zeit*, Meinecke, *Die Idee der Staats-
      räson*; and Popper, *The Open Society and its Enemies*, vol. 2,
      Chapter 12. And see Weil, *Hegel et l'État*, for the view that
      Hegel was not defending the actual Prussian setup.

28.   For a similar indictment of the poverty of the organic model
      in another of its distinctively Hegelian applications, in the
      notion of a *Zeitgeist*, see Gombrich, *Ideals and Idols*,
      24–59.

29.   Thus, the brief discussion of "corporations," which comes at
      the end of the section on civil society, argues that competing
      firms join together in such guilds by recognizing that they
      have the same selfish purposes. (Cf. Hegel, *Rechtsphilosophie*,
      Section 251). It must be said that a few passages in the *Rechts-
      philosophie* suggest a more generous view of intermediate as-
      sociations, where these are neither guilds nor organs of the
      state (ibid. Section 290, Zusatz); but they remain marginal to
      Hegel's preponderant purpose. (See also Hegel, *Enzyklopädie*,
      Section 534).

30.   No doubt the classic exposition of this argument is to be found
      in Marx's *On the Jewish Question* (in Tucker, *Marx-Engels Reader*,
      26–52). For a contemporary recitation see Macpherson, *The
      Life and Times of Liberal Democracy*, 99–100.

31.   For a representative indictment, see Arblaster, *The Rise and
      Decline of Western Liberalism*.

32.   For the contrary view, see C. Taylor, *Hegel*, 377, 387, 450–1.
      Taylor's own essay, "The Nature and Scope of Distributive
      Justice," in *Philosophical Papers*, Vol. 2, especially 311–12,
      shows more subtlety on this point. For Hegel's construal of
      the private as the realm of self-interest, see his *Rechtsphilo-
      sophie*, Sections 183, 187.

33.   Tönnies, *Gemeinschaft und Gesellschaft*; Lukacs, *Geschichte und
      Klassenbewusstsein*, which is the source of most "Western

Marxism" (cf. Jay, *Marxism and Totality*). For an example of contemporary "holism" cf. Dumont, *Essais sur l'individualisme*. A peculiarly direct expression of the Aristotelian version (cf. *Nicomachean Ethics*, 1168b31f., and also *Politics*, 1253a27, 1275a7, 1337a28) can be found in one of its medieval adherents, Remigio di Girolemi (1235–1319): "If you are not a citizen you are not a man, because a man is naturally a civil animal. ... The whole is more fully united to the part than the part is to itself." (quoted in Morrall, *Political Thought in Medieval Times*, 29).

34. Hayek, *Law, Legislation, and Liberty*, vol. 2, Chapter 10 and passim; Parsons, *The Evolution of Societies*; Luhmann, *The Differentiation of Society*, 229–54; and particularly Luhmann's critique of the whole/part metaphor of society in *Zweckbegriff und Systemrationalität*, 56ff., 171ff. Walzer's *Spheres of Justice* is a fine example of this sort of political theory.

35. Marx, "Critique of the Gotha Programme," in Tucker, *Marx–Engels Reader*, 531.

36. Marx, *Die Heilige Familie*, in Marx and Engels, *Werke*, vol. 2, 129ff. This suggests that Marx was familiar with Constant's work. Cf. his article on the historical school of law in the *Rheinische Zeitung* of 9 August 1842, where he refers to Constant's writings on religion (in *Collected Works*, vol. 1, 203–10).

37. See my earlier discussion of Herder and also the document known as *Das älteste Systemprogramme des deutschen Idealismus* (1795–7), probably composed by Hölderlin, but expressing views he then shared with Schelling and Hegel: "Die Idee der Menschheit voran – will ich zeigen, dass es keine Idee vom Staat gibt, weil der Staat etwas mechanisches ist, so wenig als es eine Idee von einer Maschine gibt. Nur was Gegenstand der Freiheit ist, heisst Idee. Wir mussen also auch über den Staat hinaus! – Denn jeder Staat muss freie Menschen als mechanisches Räderwerk behandeln" (Hölderlin, *Werke*, vol. 2, 917).

38. Marx, *Grundrisse* (1973), 488 (original German in *Grundrisse* (1939), 387); see also p. 158 on "free individuality." What I subsequently call the preconditions of freedom Marx also termed freedom within the realm of necessity, as opposed to the true realm of freedom. Cf. idem, *Capital*, vol. 3, 820. My discussion of Marx's idea of freedom is very indebted to a

paper given by Raymond Guess at the Conference on Methods (December 1983) where I presented an earlier version of this section.

39. Cf. Marx, *Capital*, III, 820; and Engels; "On Authority" (1872), reprinted in Tucker, *Marx-Engels Reader*, 730ff. In *Anti-Dühring*, Chapter 9, Engels does refer to a "proletarian morality" under communism, but without venturing any specifics.

940. Marx, *Capital*, vol. 1, Chapter IV.3. Cf. Tucker, *The Marxian Revolutionary Ideal*, Chapter 2; and Wood, "The Marxian Critique of Justice," 3–41, and "Marx on Right and Justice," 106–34.

41. *Capital*, vol. 3, 339–40. In one work of 1861–63 that he did not publish, Marx did call the worker's alienation from the means of production "ein Unrecht." See Elster, *Making Sense of Marx*, 106.

42. For an excellent treatment of this problem, see Furet, "Le jeune Marx et la révolution française," 30–46. Among Marx's early writings, see *Critique of Hegel's Philosophy of Right*, 58: "The legislature does not make the law, it merely discovers and formulates it"; and, for a particularly clear expression of this view, his article of 25 February 1849 in the *Neue Rheinische Zeitung*: " . . . Society does not depend on the law. That is a legal fiction. The law depends rather on society, it must be the expression of society's communal interests and needs, arising from the existing material mode of production. . . . It is not the Code (Napoléon) which created modern bourgeois society. Instead, it is bourgeois society, as it originated in the eighteenth century and underwent further development in the nineteenth century, which finds its merely legal expression in the Code. As soon as the Code ceases to correspond to social relations, it is no more than a bundle of paper." (in *Political Writings*, vol. 1, 250). See also the explicit and detailed statement of this view in Engel's "Zur Wohnungsfrage" (1872), in Marx and Engels, *Werke*, vol. 18, 276–77.

43. For a fine discussion of this point, see Barret-Kriegel, *L'État et les esclaves*.

44. For references and a good exposition of this point, see Buchanan, *Marx and Justice*, Chapter 4.

45. Cf. ibid., 165ff.

46. Rousseau, *Du Contrat Social*, Livre 4, Chapitre 8.
47. First half of passage from Marx, *Critique of Hegel's Philosophy of Right*, 32; second half from "On the Jewish Question," in Tucker, *Marx-Engels Reader*, 46. This commitment to overcoming the split between civil society and the state seems incompatible with Marx's simultaneous adherence to the general import of von Savigny's theory of law, namely that the state only expresses the dominant features of civil society. The contradiction does not disappear in the works of the later Marx: his theory of the state remained caught between the idea that the state is a power alienated from society and the idea that it is an organ of class rule. Cf. Tucker, *The Marxian Revolutionary Ideal*, Chapter 3; and Elster, *Making Sense of Marx*, 397–428.
48. This and the following quotations from "Critique of the Gotha Programme" appear in Tucker, *Marx-Engels Reader*, 530–1.
49. On Marx's Leibnizianism, evident in the last quotation, and its connection with the problem of distributive justice, see Elster, "Marx et Leibniz," 167–77.
50. Cf. Elster, *Making Sense of Marx*, 221f.
51. From the Right, Scruton (*The Meaning of Conservativism*, 72) charges that liberalism rests essentially upon Kantian individualism. For a similar complaint on the Left see, besides my discussion of Sandel below, MacIntyre, *After Virtue*, 182. With the rise of antiliberal communitarianism among writers who situate themselves on the Left, the very distinction between Right and Left has become obscure. Perhaps it is a matter of whether the desirable community is thought to be already existent or yet to be achieved. But this does not clearly fit Leftist communitarians such as MacIntyre or Sandel.
52. Rawls, *A Theory of Justice*, 560ff. See also Rawls, "Reply to Alexander and Musgrave," 641.
53. Rawls, *A Theory of Justice*, 251ff.
54. Ibid., 574.
55. Ibid., 264; and idem, "The Basic Structure as Subject," 165.
56. Sandel, *Liberalism and the Limits of Justice*, 1ff.
57. Ibid., 79f., 94f.
58. At this point Sandel turns away from an adequate examination of the one expressivist strand of liberalism that concerns him. While insisting that the Kantian notion of moral personhood

is empty unless transcendental, he offers no reasons to reject a transcendental subject, only a passing reference to its "obscurity and arbitrariness" and to "metaphysical embarrassment" (ibid., 13–14, 37). In the previous chapter I tried to pinpoint what is wrong with Kant's belief that we must understand ourselves as having an empirically unconditioned sense of duty if we are to view ourselves as moral beings.

59. Ibid., 62, 179.

60. Yet it cannot be right to say, as Sandel does, that Kantians lack any notion of character, since for them "no transformation of my aims and attachments could call into question the person I am" (ibid., 179). If moral character means an unwillingness to conceive of one's life without the commitment to honor one's duties toward others, it plays an intrinsic role in Kant's *Tugendlehre*. What is wrong in Kant's ethics is not that it has nothing to say about character, but rather that it gives an inadequate account of it.

61. Ibid., 7, 11, 47–9, 65.

62. Ibid., 179–83.

63. Cf. Rawls, *A Theory of Justice*, 126f., 138f., and also 569, 584.

64. This is contrary to the view of Scanlon in "Rawls's Theory of Justice," 1020–69 (reprinted in revised form in *Reading Rawls*, 169–205).

65. This implies that any beliefs that all people do happen to share about the good should be allowed to figure behind the veil of ignorance. Perhaps here we have a fruitful way of understanding Rawls's theory of "primary goods" (wealth, income, self-respect, liberty, etc.): They will be desired, not necessarily by anyone having any conception of the good at all, but rather by anyone having one of the conceptions of the good that appear in modern pluralistic societies. Cf. Rawls, "Social Unity and Primary Goods," 159–85.

66. This criticism of Rawls appears not only among antiliberals, but also in liberal writers such as Walzer, *Spheres of Justice*, 5. For the idea that equal respect underlies the force of reasoning from the original position, see Dworkin's *Taking Rights Seriously*, 150–83.

67. Rawls, "Kantian Constructivism in Moral Theory," 544. I cannot understand how Galston ("Moral Personality and Liberal Theory," 492ff.) could have come to the opposite conclusion,

that the "Dewey Lectures" resolve the tension between Kantian and modus vivendi justifications in favor of the former.

68. Rawls, "Kantian Constructivism in Moral Theory," 545. This clarification in Rawls's thought is now explicit in his essay "Justice as Fairness: Political, not Metaphysical," 223–51.

69. Sandel, *Liberalism and the Limits of Justice*, 30, 40.

70. Ibid., 182.

71. *Ibid.*, 32ff., 180ff. The same fantasy has appealed to another contemporary antiliberal on the Left. Cf. MacIntyre, *After Virtue*, 147: "Indeed from an Aristotelian point of view a modern liberal political society can appear only as a collection of citizens of nowhere who have banded together for their common protection. They possess at best that inferior form of friendship which is founded on mutual advantage. That they lack the bond of friendship is of course bound up with the self-avowed moral pluralism of such liberal societies." For a masterly, empirically based study of the possibilities of community, see M. Taylor, *Community, Anarchy, and Liberty*, 26–32. Taylor shows that if by "community" we mean a group having beliefs and values in common, relations among its members that are direct and many-sided, and a system of reciprocity, then it will have to be small and stable.

72. Cf. Scruton, *The Meaning of Conservatism*, 50 and passim; and Will, *Statecraft as Soulcraft*.

73. Sandel, op. cit., 36f. Cf. Kant, "Idea of a Universal History," Sections 4f., which is noted by Rawls, *A Theory of Justice*, 257.

74. Sandel, op. cit., 78ff., 85ff. Cf. Rawls, *A Theory of Justice*, 179.

75. Sandel, op. cit., 96. Cf. Nozick, *Anarchy, State, and Utopia*, 213ff., 228ff.

76. Sandel, op. cit., 1, 79ff., 101ff., 134, 143–54, 178.

77. Cf., for example, Locke, *A Letter Concerning Toleration*, 45: "The business of laws is not to provide for the truth of opinions, but for the safety and security of the commonwealth, and of every particular man's goods and person." Obviously, Locke thought that the truth of opinions (including theological ones, cf. his *The Reasonableness of Christianity*) was of the greatest import in other areas of social life.

78. In certain regards this position resembles closely that of Schumpeter, *Capitalism, Socialism, and Democracy*, 232–302,

which views democracy as a method rather than an ultimate value, because it recognizes that the common good is an object of dispute. But none of this implies Schumpeter's "economical model of democracy," according to which democracy is simply a matter of leaders competing for votes, and which I do not accept. Ideals remain important. Liberal democracy requires the pursuit of neutrality and permits the pursuit of agreed-upon ideals; it also allows for efforts to persuade others of the cogency of one's own ideals.

CHAPTER 6. THE HETEROGENEITY OF MORALITY

1. It is this foundationalist perspective that unites Sartre's moral subjectivism (cf. *L'existentialisme est un humanisme*) and Alasdair MacIntyre's wish for a return to a teleological view of man in *After Virtue*. See Chapter 2 of this book.

2. For a similar distinction see Nagel, *The View from Nowhere*, 162–6. Nagel's discussion, which appeared earlier in his Tanner Lectures "The Limits of Objectivity," is one to which I am very indebted (see below). I shall follow Nagel and Bernard Williams in using the term "consequentialism" for the position so described in the text. This differs somewhat from its traditional use in ethics (i.e., the doctrine that the worth of an action depends on the worth of its consequences), while still remaining connected with it: "Consequentialism" requires, we shall see, that in determining what I ought to do I should take into account what others are likely to do as a consequence of what I do. For more on this, see below.

3. A cautionary note about how I shall be using "reasons" in this essay: (1) In referring to the reasons an agent has for some action, I shall be assuming that he acknowledges these as reasons; (2) such reasons need not be decisive ones for him.

4. Butler, *Fifteen Sermons Preached at the Rolls Chapel*, in *Analogy of Religion and Sermons*, Preface: paragraphs 15ff., 24f.; Sermon

I: paragraphs 6–8. Subsequent references to the *Sermons* will be in the text and will give the number of the sermon in Roman numerals and of the paragraph in Arabic numerals. References to his *Dissertation upon the Nature of Virtue*, also found in *Analogy of Religion and Sermons*, will be abbreviated DNV and will contain the paragraph number.

5. See the discussion in Williams "A Critique of Utilitarianism," in Williams and Smart, *Utilitarianism: For and Against*, 93–118. The terms "agent-centered prerogative" and "agent-centered restriction" come from Scheffler, *The Rejection of Consequentialism*.

6. Butler, DNV:8: "The fact then appears to be that we are constituted so as to condemn falsehood, unprovoked violence, injustice, and to approve of benevolence to some, preferably to others, abstracted from all consideration which conduct is likeliest to produce an overbalance of happiness or misery. And therefore, were the Author of Nature to propose nothing to himself as an end but the production of happiness, were his moral character merely that of benevolence, yet ours is not so. Upon that supposition, indeed, the only reason of his giving us the above-mentioned approbation of benevolence to some persons rather than to others, and disapprobation of falsehood, unprovoked violence, and injustice, must be that he foresaw this constitution of our nature would produce more happiness than forming us with a temper of mere general benevolence." See also XII:31 (footnote) where Butler clearly accepts this "supposition." On the traditional idea of the divine administration of morality, see Schneewind, "The Divine Corporation and the History of Ethics," 173–91.

7. Cf. Williams, op. cit., 81, 125. I should observe that indirect consequentialism is not the same as rule-consequentialism (the view that that action is morally best that is recommended by a rule the general observance of which brings about more good overall than any other rule), since a rule-consequentialist might still hold that agents should take this greater good as their motive for heeding the rule.

8. Sidgwick, *The Methods of Ethics*, 413. Sidgwick concluded, of course, that a similarly secular reconciliation of egoism and universal benevolence was impossible. His recognition of the

"dualism of practical reason" was at least part of the way toward the truth.

9. Butler's influence on the nineteenth century debate between intuitionism and utilitarianism is excellently presented in Schneewind, *Sidgwick's Ethics and Victorian Moral Philosophy*.

10. The traditional distinction between the intrinsically and the instrumentally good is orthogonal to the four categories listed above: goods of each of the categories (or at least of the first three) can be either intrinsically or instrumentally valuable (or both).

11. In this discussion of urgency I am much indebted to Scanlon's "Preference and Urgency," 655–69, although I believe that this notion must be connected not only with the idea of objectivity (as he does), but also with that of unanimity. Thus, in a society founded on toleration, I may be convinced that my preference for X is for something objectively good, and yet feel no urgency to ensure that you get X, too (X may be the last thing you want).

12. The consequentialist view of friendship can be found in Sidgwick, op. cit., 430–9. See the insightful critique of such a view in Stocker, "The Schizophrenia of Modern Ethical Theories," 453–66.

13. This seems to be the suggestion in Williams, *Moral Luck*, 14: "A man who has a ground project will be required by Utilitarianism to give up what he requires in a given case just if that conflicts with what he is required to do as an impersonal utility-maximizer when all the causally relevant considerations are in. That is a quite absurd requirement. But the Kantian, who can do rather better than this, still cannot do well enough. For impartial morality, if the conflict really does arise, must be required to win; and that cannot necessarily be a reasonable demand on the agent." It is even clearer in Wolf, "Moral Saints," 419–39, especially 431–2.

14. See several of the papers by Aurel Kolnai, collected in *Ethics, Value and Reality*. This difference between consequentialism and deontology ("intuitionism") is also recognized by Sidgwick (op. cit., 87), although he proceeds to reject the latter.

15. Weber, *Politik als Beruf*, 66: "Insofern sind Gesinnungsethik und Verantwortungsethik nicht absolut Gegensätze, sondern Ergänzungen, die zusammen erst den echten Menschen ausmachen, den, der den 'Beruf zur Politik' haben kann."

16. Kant, "Über ein vermeintes Recht," 426, 428: "Wahrhaftigkeit in Aussagen, die man nicht umgehen kann, ist formale Pflicht des Menschen gegen jeden, es mag ihm oder einem andern daraus auch noch so grosser Nachteil erwachsen. . . . Er selbst *tut* also hiermit dem, der dadurch leidet, eigentlich nicht Schaden, sondern diesen *verursacht* der Zufall." In this passage, "Nachteil" denotes disadvantage, not loss of moral value.

17. Nagel, *The View from Nowhere*, 152f., 164ff. Sometimes Nagel describes both sorts of reasons as capable of objectivity (153, 162); yet oddly at other times he associates only consequentialist reasons with "the objective point of view" (180, 183). For my part I must say that consequentialist reasons seem no more "objective" in any interesting sense than deontological ones. The fact that we have deontological duties is no less an item of reasoned agreement than the fact that we have consequentialist ones.

18. Cf. Frankena, *Ethics*, 14ff.

19. Cf., Sidgwick, *Methods of Ethics*, 382.

20. Cf. Levi; *Hard Choices: Decision-making under Unresolved Conflict*, Chapter 2.

21. Williams ("Ethical Consistency," in *Problems of the Self*) has argued that to understand irresolvable moral conflict we must give up, not "ought" implies "can," but rather the "agglomeration principle" – namely, that if I ought to do A and I ought to do B, then I ought to do A and B. I do not think that this is right. It is true (as Williams points out) that the similar agglomeration principle for "desirable" fails: It may be desirable to do A and desirable to do B without it being desirable to do A and B. But when this is so, it is because doing A makes doing B undesirable. Generally, there is no parallel reason for rejecting agglomeration in the case of the moral "ought": Doing A does not, in the case of irresolvable moral conflict, make B cease to be obligatory.

22. Perhaps the dissimilarity between moral and scientific reasoning will not seem so great, if we consider common-sense

judgments such as "I have two hands." Too certain for any other beliefs to justify, they function not so much as background knowledge as rather the conditions for being a "knowing subject" at all.

Bibliography

Ackerman, Bruce A. *Social Justice in the Liberal State*. New Haven: Yale University Press, 1980.

"What is Neutral about Neutrality?." *Ethics* 93 (January 1983): 372–90.

Ackrill, J. L. "Aristotle on *Eudaimonia*." In *Essays on Aristotle's Ethics*. Edited by A. O. Rorty. Berkeley and Los Angeles: University of California Press, 1980.

Adorno, Theodor W., and Horkheimer, Max. *Dialectic of the Enlightenment*. Translated by John Cumming. New York: Continuum, 1982. (Original German edition published in 1944.)

Aquinas, St. Thomas. *Summa Theologica*. 60 vols. London: Eyre and Spottiswoode, 1963–75.

Arblaster, Anthony. *The Rise and Decline of Western Liberalism*. Oxford: Basil Blackwell, 1984.

Arendt, Hannah. *The Human Condition*. Chicago: University of Chicago Press, 1958.

The Origins of Totalitarianism. New York: Harcourt Brace Jovanovich, 1973.

Aristotle. *Ethica Nicomachea*. Edited by I. Bywater. Oxford: Oxford University Press, 1970.

Eudemian Ethics. The Athenian Constitution. On Virtues and Vices. Edited by H. Rackham. Cambridge, Mass.: Harvard University Press, 1971.

De Motu Animalium. Edited by Martha C. Nussbaum. Princeton: Princeton University Press, 1978.

Politica. Edited by W. D. Ross. Oxford: Oxford University Press, 1962.

[Aristotle]. *Magna Moralia*. Edited by G. C. Armstrong. Cambridge, Mass.: Harvard University Press, 1962.

Bibliography

Avineri, Shlomo. *Hegel's Theory of the Modern State.* Cambridge: Cambridge University Press, 1972.

Barret-Kriegel, Blandine. *L'Etat et les esclaves.* Paris: Calmann-Lévy, 1979.

Barry, Brian. *Political Argument.* London: Routledge and Kegan Paul, 1965.

Bayle, Pierre. *Commentaire philosophique sur ces paroles de Jésus-Christ: "Contrains-les d'entrer"* (1686), in *Oeuvres diverses.* Paris: Editions sociales, 1971.

Beck, L. W. *Commentary on Kant's Critique of Practical Reason.* Chicago: University of Chicago Press, 1960.

Berlin, Isaiah. *Concepts and Categories.* Harmondsworth, U.K.: Penguin, 1981.

Four Essays on Liberty. Oxford: Oxford University Press, 1969.

Vico and Herder. New York: Viking, 1976.

Bittner, Rüdiger, and Cramer, Konrad, eds. *Materialien zu Kants Kritik der praktischen Vernunft.* Frankfurt: Suhrkamp, 1975.

Bodin, Jean. *Les Six Livres de la République.* Paris: du Puys, 1583.

Bradley, F. H. *Ethical Studies.* Indianapolis: Bobbs-Merrill, 1951.

Buchanan, Allan E. *Marx and Justice.* Totowa, N.J.: Rowman and Littlefield, 1982.

Butler, Joseph. *Analogy of Religion and Sermons.* London: Bohn, 1855.

Cassirer, Ernst. *The Question of Jean-Jacques Rousseau.* New York: Columbia University Press, 1954. (Original German edition published in 1932.)

Rousseau, Kant, Goethe. Princeton: Princeton University Press, 1945.

Constant, Benjamin. *De la Liberté chez les Modernes.* Edited by M. Gauchet. Paris: Librairie générale française, 1980.

Darwall, Stephen L. "Two Kinds of Respect." *Ethics* 88, 1 (October 1977): 36–49.

Dent, N. J. H. *The Moral Psychology of the Virtues.* Cambridge: Cambridge University Press, 1984.

Dumont, Louis. *Essais sur l'individualisme.* Paris: Seuil, 1983.

Durkheim, Emile. *Leçons de Sociologie.* Paris: Presses Universitaires de France, 1950.

Dworkin, Ronald. "Liberalism." In *Public and Private Morality,* edited by Stuart Hampshire. Princeton: Princeton University Press, 1978.

Taking Rights Seriously. Cambridge, Mass.: Harvard University Press, 1978.

Bibliography

Elster, Jon. *Making Sense of Marx*. Cambridge: Cambridge University Press, 1985.

"Marx et Leibniz." *Revue Philosophique* 1983(2): 167–77.

Engels, Friedrich. *Anti-Dühring*. Peking: Foreign Language Press, 1976.

Fichte, J. G. *Schriften zur Revolution*. Edited by B. Willms. Frankfurt, Berlin, Wien: Ullstein, 1973.

Finnis, John. *Natural Law and Natural Rights*. Oxford: Oxford University Press, 1980.

Foot, Philippa. *Virtues and Vices*. Berkeley: University of California Press, 1978.

Frankena, William. *Ethics*. 2d ed. Englewood Cliffs: Prentice-Hall, 1973.

"Obligation and Motivation in Recent Moral Philosophy." In *Essays in Moral Philosophy*, edited by A. I. Melden. Seattle: University of Washington Press, 1958.

Furet, François. "Le Jeune Marx et la révolution française." *Le Débat* 28 (janvier 1984): 30–46.

Gadamer, Hans-Georg. *Kleine Schriften*. Band I. Tübingen, Germany: Mohr, 1967.

"Rhetorik, Hermeneutik und Ideologiekritik." In Hermeneutik und Ideologiekritik, edited by K. O. Apel, et al. Frankfurt: Suhrkamp, 1971.

Wahrheit und Methode. Tübingen, Germany: Mohr, 1960.

Galston, William. "Moral Personality and Liberal Theory." *Political Theory* 10, 4 (November 1982): 492–519.

Gay, Peter. *The Enlightenment*. 2 vols. New York: Norton, 1969.

Geuss, Raymond. *The Idea of a Critical Theory*. Cambridge: Cambridge University Press, 1981.

Gombrich, E. H. *Ideals and Idols*. Oxford: Phaidon, 1979.

Guicciardini, Francesco. *Ricordi*. Edited by E. Pasquini. Milano: Garzanti, 1975.

Habermas, Jürgen. *Communication and the Evolution of Society*. Boston: Beacon Press, 1979.

"Reply to My Critics," in *Habermas: Critical Debates*, edited by J. B. Thompson and D. Held. Cambridge, Mass.: MIT Press, 1982.

Strukturwandel der Öffentlichkeit. Darmstadt, Germany: Luchterhand, 1962.

Theorie des kommunikativen Handelns. 2 vols. Frankfurt: Suhrkamp, 1981.

Theorie und Praxis. Frankfurt: Suhrkamp, 1971.

Vorstudien und Ergänzungen zur Theorie des kommunikativen Handelns. Frankfurt: Suhrkamp, 1984.

Habermas, Jürgen, and Luhmann, Niklas. *Theorie der Gesellschaft oder Sozialtechnologie*. Frankfurt: Suhrkamp, 1971.

Hampshire, Stuart. *Morality and Conflict*. Cambridge, Mass.: Harvard University Press, 1983.

Hayek, Friedrich. *Law, Legislation, and Liberty*. 3 vols. Chicago: University of Chicago Press, 1976.

Haym, Rudolf. *Hegel und seine Zeit*. Berlin: Gaertner, 1857.

Hegel, G. F. W. *Briefe*. 4 vols. Edited by J. Hoffmeister. Hamburg: Meiner, 1969–81.

Enzyklopädie der philosophischen Wissenschaften. 3d ed. Berlin, 1830.

Jenaer Schriften. Frankfurt: Suhrkamp, 1980.

Natural Law. Translated by T. M. Knox. Philadelphia: University of Pennsylvania Press, 1975.

Phänomenologie des Geistes. Hamburg: Meiner, 1952.

Reason in History. Translated by R. S. Hartman. Indianapolis: Bobbs-Merrill. 1953.

Grundlinien der Philosophie des Rechts (also known as *Rechtsphilosophie*). Berlin: Nicolai, 1821.

Schriften zur Politik und Rechtsphilosophie. 2d ed. Edited by G. Lanson. Leipzig: Meiner, 1923.

Theologische Jugendschriften. Edited by H. Nohl. Tübingen, Germany: Mohr, 1907.

Vorlesungen über die Geschichte der Philosophie. 3 vols. Frankfurt: Suhrkamp, 1971.

Vorlesungen über die Philosophie der Geschichte. Frankfurt: Suhrkamp, 1971.

Herder, J. G. *Abhandlung über den Ursprung der Sprache*. 2d ed. Berlin: Voss, 1789.

Auch eine Philosophie der Geschichte zur Bildung der Menschheit. Frankfurt: Suhrkamp, 1967.

Briefe zu Beförderung der Humanitat. Riga: Hartknoch, 1793–97.

Ideen zur Philosophie der Geschichte der Menschheit. Riga: Hartknoch, 1784.

Sämtliche Werke. Edited by B. Suphan. 33 vols. Berlin: Weidmann, 1877–1913.

Hölderlin, Friedrich. *Werke*. Darmstadt, Germany: Wissenschaftliche Buchgesellschaft, 1970.

Holmes, O. W. *The Common Law*. Boston: Heath, 1881.

Bibliography

Holmes, Stephen T. *Benjamin Constant and the Making of Modern Liberalism*. New Haven: Yale University Press, 1984.

Hume, David. *An Inquiry Concerning the Principles of Morals*. In *Hume's Enquiries*, edited by L. A. Selby-Bige. Oxford: Oxford University Press, 1902.

Treatise of Human Nature. Edited by L. A. Selby-Bige. Oxford: Oxford University Press, 1965.

Hyppolite, Jean. *Introduction à la philosophie de l'histoire de Hegel*. Paris: Nagel, 1948.

Jay, Martin. *Marxism and Totality*. Berkeley and Los Angeles: University of California Press, 1984.

Kant, Immanuel. *Critique of Practical Reason*. Translated by L. W. Beck. Indianapolis: Bobbs-Merrill, 1960.

Groundwork of the Metaphysics of Morals. Translated by H. J. Paton. London: Hutchinson, 1956.

Grundlegung zur Metaphysik der Sitten. Berlin: Preussische Akademie der Wissenschaften ("Akademie-Ausgabe"), Band IV, 1900ff.

Kritik der praktischen Vernunft. Berlin: Akademie-Ausgabe, Band V, 1900ff.

Kritik der reinen Vernunft. Riga: Hartknoch, 1781 and 1787.

Lectures on Ethics. Translated by L. Infield. London: Methuen, 1979.

Die Metaphysik der Sitten. 1st ed. Königsberg: Nicolai, 1797. (2d ed. Königsberg: Nicolai, 1798)

Die Religion innerhalb der Grenzen der blossen Vernunft. 2d ed. Königsberg: Nicolai, 1794.

"Über den Gemeinspruch: das mag in der Theorie richtig sein, taugt aber nicht für die Praxis." *Berlinische Monatsschrift* (September 1793): 201–84.

"Über ein vermeintes Recht aus Menschenliebe zu lügen." in *Gesammelte Schriften*, Band VIII. Berlin: Akademie-Ausgabe, 1910.

Kelly, George Armstrong. *Hegel's Retreat from Eleusis*. Princeton: Princeton University Press, 1978.

Kolnai, Aurel. *Ethics, Value and Reality*. Indianapolis: Hackett, 1978.

Kuhn, T. S. *The Essential Tension*. Chicago: Chicago University Press, 1977.

Levi, Isaac. *Hard Choices. Decision-making under Unresolved Conflict* Cambridge: Cambridge University Press, 1986.

Locke, John. *A Letter Concerning Toleration.* Indianapolis: Bobbs-Merrill, 1955. (Original edition published in 1689.)
> *The Reasonableness of Christianity.* London: Churchill, 1696.

Luhmann, Niklas. *The Differentiation of Society.* Translated by S. Holmes and C. Larmore. New York: Columbia University Press, 1982.
> "The Improbability of Communication." *International Social Science Journal* 33, 1 (1981): 122–32.
> *Zweckbegriff und Systemrationalität.* Frankfurt: Suhrkamp, 1973.

Lukacs, Georg. *Geschichte und Klassenbewusstsein.* Neuwied and Berlin: Luchterhand, 1968.

Lukes, Steven. "Of Gods and Demons: Habermas and Practical Reason." In *Habermas: Critical Debates,* edited by J. B. Thompson and D. Held. Cambridge, Mass.: MIT Press, 1982.

McDowell, John. "The Role of Eudaimonia in Aristotle's Ethics." In *Essays on Aristotle's Ethics,* edited by A. O. Rorty. Berkeley and Los Angeles: University of California Press, 1980.

MacIntyre, Alasdair. *After Virtue.* London: Duckworth, 1981.
> "How Moral Agents Became Ghosts." *Synthese* 53 (1982): 295–312.
> "The Magic in the Pronoun 'My.' " *Ethics* (October 1983): 113–25.

Macpherson, C. B. *The Life and Times of Liberal Democracy.* Oxford: Oxford University Press, 1977.

Madison, James; Hamilton, Alexander; and Jay, John. *The Federalist.* New York: Modern Library, 1937.

Marx, Karl. *Capital.* 3 vols. New York: International Publishers, 1967.
> *Collected Works.* 41 vols. New York: International Publishers, 1975–85.
> *Critique of Hegel's Philosophy of Right.* Cambridge: Cambridge University Press, 1972.
> *Grundrisse.* Moscow: Verlag für fremdsprachige Literatur, 1938.
> *Grundrisse.* Translated by M. Nicolaus. New York: Vintage, 1973.
> *Political Writings.* 3 vols. New York: Vintage, 1974.

Marx, Karl, and Engels, Friedrich. *Werke.* 39 vols. Berlin: Dietz, 1956–67.

Meinecke, Friedrich. *Die Idee der Staatsräson.* Berlin: Oldenbourg, 1925.

Mill, J. S. *Utilitarianism. On Liberty. Representative Government.* London: Dent, 1972.

Bibliography

Montesqueiu, Charles Louis de Secondat de. *Oeuvres Complètes.* 2 vols. Paris: Gallimard, 1951.

Morrall, John B. *Political Thought in Medieval Times.* New York: Harper & Row, 1958.

Müller, Adam. *Elemente der Staatskunst.* Berlin: Sander, 1809.

Nagel, Thomas. "The Limits of Objectivity." In *The Tanner Lectures on Human Values.* Salt Lake City: University of Utah Press, 1980.

Mortal Questions. Cambridge: Cambridge University Press, 1979.

The Possibility of Altruism. Princeton: Princeton University Press, 1970.

The View from Nowhere. New York: Oxford University Press, 1986.

Novalis. *Werke.* 2 vols. Edited by H. J. Mähl and R. Samuel. Munich: Hanser, 1978.

Nozick, Robert. *Anarchy, State, and Utopia.* New York: Basic Books, 1974.

Oakeshott, Michael. *Rationalism in Politics and Other Essays.* London: Methuen, 1962.

Paine, Thomas. *Rights of Man (1791–92).* Harmondsworth, U.K.: Penguin, 1984.

Parsons, Talcott. *The Evolution of Societies.* Englewood Cliffs: Prentice-Hall, 1977.

Plant, Raymond. *Hegel.* 2d ed. Oxford: Blackwells, 1983.

Plutarch. *De Virtute Morali.* In *Moralia,* vol. 6. Edited by W. C. Helmbold. Cambridge, Mass.: Harvard University Press, 1939.

Pocock, J. G. A. *Virtue, Commerce, and History.* Cambridge: Cambridge University Press, 1985.

Popper, Karl. *The Open Society and its Enemies.* 5th ed. 2 vols. Princeton: Princeton University Press, 1966.

Prichard, H. A. *Moral Obligation.* Oxford: Oxford University Press, 1968.

Rawls, John. "The Basic Structure as Subject." *American Philosophical Quarterly* 14 (1977): 159–65.

"Justice as Fairness: Political, not Metaphysical." *Philosophy and Public Affairs* 14, 3 (Summer 1985): 223–51.

"Kantian Constructivism in Moral Theory. The John Dewey Lectures." *Journal of Philosophy* 77, 9 (September 1980): 515–72.

"Reply to Alexander and Musgrave." *Quarterly Journal of Economics* 88 (November 1974): 633–55.

"Social Unity and Primary Goods." In *Utilitarianism and Beyond,* edited by A. Sen and B. Williams. Cambridge: Cambridge University Press, 1982.

Reiss, Hans. *The Political Thought of the German Romantics*. Oxford: Oxford University Press, 1955.

Ritter, Joachim. *Metaphysik und Politik*. Frankfurt: Suhrkamp, 1969.

Rousseau, J. J. *Du Contrat Social*, in *Oeuvres Complètes*, vol. 3. Paris: Gallimard. 1964.

Ryle, Gilbert. *The Concept of Mind*. New York: Barnes and Noble, 1949.

Sandel, Michael. *Liberalism and the Limits of Justice*. Cambridge: Cambridge University Press, 1982.

Sartre, Jean-Paul. *L'Existentialisme est un humanisme*. Paris: Nagel, 1946.

Scanlon, T. M. "Preference and Urgency." *Journal of Philosophy* 72 (1975): 655–69.

  "Rawls's Theory of Justice." *University of Pennsylvania Law Review* 121 (1973): 1020–69.

  "Rawls's Theory of Justice." In *Reading Rawls*, edited by N. Daniels. Oxford: Blackwell's, 1975.

Scheffler, Samuel. *The Rejection of Consequentialism*. Oxford: Oxford University Press, 1982.

Schiller, Friedrich. *Schriften zur Philosophie und Kunst*. Munich: Goldmann, 1964.

Schlanger, Judith E. *Les Métaphores de l'organisme*. Paris: Vrin, 1971.

Schlegel, Freidrich von. *Athenäumsfragmente* (1798). In *Schriften zur Literatur*. Munich: Hanser, 1970.

Schneewind, J. B. "The Divine Corporation and the History of Ethics." In *Philosophy in History*. Edited by R. Rorty, J. B. Schneewind, and Q. Skinner. Cambridge: Cambridge University Press, 1984.

  Sidgwick's Ethics and Victorian Moral Philosophy. Oxford: Oxford University Press, 1977.

  "Virtue, Narrative, and Community." *Journal of Philosophy* 79, 2 (November 1982): 653–63.

Schumpeter, Joseph. *Capitalism, Socialism, and Democracy*. New York: Harper and Brothers, 1942.

Scruton, Roger. *The Meaning of Conservatism*. Harmondsworth, U.K.: Penguin, 1980.

Seneca. *Letters from a Stoic*. Translated by R. Campbell. Harmondsworth: Penguin, 1969.

Sidgwick, Henry. *The Methods of Ethics*. 7th ed. London: Macmillan, 1907.

Bibliography

Smith, Adam. *The Theory of Moral Sentiments*. Indianapolis: Liberty Classics, 1969.

Stocker, Michael. "The Schizophrenia of Modern Ethical Theories." *Journal of Philosophy* 73 (1976): 453–66.

Strauss, Leo. *Natural Right and History*. Chicago: Chicago University Press, 1953.

Taylor, Charles. *Hegel*. Cambridge: Cambridge University Press, 1975.

Philosophical Papers. 2 vols. Cambridge: Cambridge University Press, 1985.

Taylor, Michael. *Community, Anarchy, and Liberty*. Cambridge: Cambridge University Press, 1982.

Tönnies, Friedrich. *Gemeinschaft und Gesellschaft*. Leipzig: Fues, 1887.

Tucker, Robert C. *The Marxian Revolutionary Ideal*. New York: Norton, 1969.

ed. *Marx–Engels Reader*. New York: Norton, 1978.

Tugendhat, Ernst. *Probleme der Ethik*. Stuttgart: Reclam, 1984.

Walzer, Michael. "Liberalism and the Art of Separation." *Political Theory* 12, 3 (August 1984): 315–30.

Spheres of Justice. New York: Basic Books, 1983.

Warnock, G. J. *The Object of Morality*. London: Methuen, 1971.

Weber, Max. *Politik als Beruf*. Sechste Auflage. Berlin: Duncker und Humblot, 1977.

Wirtschaft und Gesellschaft. Tübingen, Germany: Mohr, 1972.

Weil, Eric. *Hegel et l'État*. Paris: Vrin, 1950.

Will, George. *Statecraft as Soulcraft*. New York: Simon and Schuster, 1983.

Williams, Bernard. *Ethics and the Limits of Philosophy*. Cambridge, Mass.: Harvard University Press, 1985.

Moral Luck. Cambridge: Cambridge University Press, 1981.

Problems of the Self. Cambridge: Cambridge University Press, 1973.

Williams, Bernard, and Smart, J. J. C. *Utilitarianism: For and Against*. Cambridge: Cambridge University Press, 1973.

Wolf, Susan. "Moral Saints." *Journal of Philosophy* 79 (1982): 419–39.

Wood, Allen. "The Marxian Critique of Justice." In *Marx, Justice and History*, edited by M. Cohen, T. Nagel, and T. Scanlon. Princeton: Princeton University Press, 1980.

"Marx on Right and Justice." In *Marx, Justice and History*, edited by M. Cohen, T. Nagel, and T. Scanlon. Princeton: Princeton University Press, 1980.

Index

Adorno, Theodor W., 25
alienation, 76, 93, 103
antiliberalism, viii, xi, 22–3, 70, 76, 92, 93, 103, 105–6, 119, 129
Aquinas, St. Thomas, 159 n23, 159 n29
Arblaster, Anthony, 170 n31
Arendt, Hannah, 25, 29, 108
Aristotle: and character, 15, 81, 86–7, 89, 101–2; and the good life, 23, 34–9, 158 n19, 159 n22–23; and judgment, ix, 1, 5, 15–16, 37; and moral conflict, 10, 37–8, 159 n29; and virtue, 11–12, 30, 31–4; and whole/part model of society, 96, 105, 107
attachments, see ties, constitutive
autonomy, see Kant, Immanuel, and autonomy

Barry, Brian, 160 n5
Bayle, Pierre, 76, 123, 130
belonging, see Sittlichkeit
Bentham, Jeremy, 26, 27, 37, 48
Berlin, Isaiah, 38–9, 47, 166 n4
Bodin, Jean, x, 76, 130
Bradley, F. H., 132–3, 168 n20
Burke, Edmund, 99
Butler, Joseph, 31, 32, 133, 134–9, 145

capitalism, 71, 107, 109, 112
character, see Aristotle, and character; Sittlichkeit
citizen (citoyen) versus homme, 75–6, 93, 105, 110, 114, 116, 117, 123, 125
communitarianism, 92, 93, 104, 123, 128, 175 n71
conflict, moral, 9–11, 38–9, 133, 137–8, 144, 155 n7; irresolvable, ix, 11, 133, 149–50
Constant, Benjamin, 47, 145, 167 n12, 169 n24, 171 n36

democracy, 130, 176 n78
differentiation, social, viii, xi, 92–3, 97, 98, 99, 105, 106–7, 114, 115, 116, 117, 118, 123, 125, 129–30
Durkheim, Emile, 160 n6
duties, see obligations
Dworkin, Ronald, 62, 162 n17, 174 n66

Elster, Jon, 173 n49
Enlightenment, 25, 26, 28, 30, 31–3, 93, 99, 166 n1, 166 n3
ethics (see also morality; obligations): of conviction, xi, 144–9; Greek, ix, 38, 41–2, 78, 163 n9; modern and its strengths and weaknesses, 4–5, 12, 16–17, 34–5; of responsibility, xii, 144–9; of virtue versus ethics of duty, 11–12
examples, moral, 1–2, 8, 21
experimentalism, viii, 51, 52, 55, 66, 74
expressivism, political, 73, 76, 83, 90, 91, 120, 121, 123, 129, 164 n20, 167 n8; antiliberal forms of, 76–7, 92–3, 96, 97, 98–9, 103–4, 106, 114, 115, 119, 123

Fichte, J. G., 82, 165 n22
fragmentation, see whole/part model of society
freedom, viii, 45, 46–7, 108–9, 113, 117; and bureaucracy, 40–2, 157 n5, 160 n6; see also Kant, Immanuel, and autonomy
friendship, 79, 126, 132, 141, 144, 163 n10

Gadamer, Hans-Georg, 18–19
Geuss, Raymond, 171 n38
good: kinds of, 139–41, 178 n10; see also right
Guicciardini, Francesco, 17

Habermas, Jürgen, 19, 55–8, 161 n12
Hampshire, Stuart, xi
Hayek, Friedrich, 107
Hegel, G. F. W., 65, 92, 99–106, 118, 119, 120, 123, 168 n14, 169 n23, 170 n26, 170 n29, 171 n37

Index

Helvétius, Claude, 32, 94
Herder, J. G., 92, 93–8, 99, 100, 104, 106, 115, 118, 167 n5
heterogeneity of morality, viii–ix, x, xii, 38, 138, 145, 148, 151
Hobbes, Thomas, 32
Holbach, Baron, 94
Hölderlin, Friedrich, 171 n37
Horkheimer, Max, 25
humanism, civic, 160 n4
Hume, David, 26, 27, 62, 70–2, 73, 112, 120, 123, 163 n4
Hutcheson, Francis, 72, 135

ideals: personal, xi, 69, 70, 73–4, 76, 77, 92, 95, 106, 119, 122, 129, 152–3, see also Kant, Immanuel, and autonomy; substantial, 73–4, 75, 76, 80, 93, 96, 97
individualism, 25, 34, 106, 126
individuality, 21, 94, 113

judgment, vii, ix, 7, 14, 40–2, 138, 148, 151, 152; and rules, 5, 7–8, 155 n6; and two sorts of duties, 5–6, 11, 13; two tasks of, 6, 9; and virtue, 11–14; see also conflict, moral
justice, 45–6, 69, 108–13, 115–8, 120–9; circumstances of, 70–3, 112, 120, 124, 126

Kant, Immanuel: and autonomy, viii, 51–2, 55, 66, 70, 74, 76, 77–83, 90, 91–2, 94, 95, 97, 101, 102, 103, 104, 106, 118, 120, 122, 123, 124, 127, 129, 143, 158 n18, 164 n20, 166 n31; and empirically unconditioned interest in morality, 31, 80–6, 88, 90, 100, 101, 102, 103, 122, 127; and ethics of conviction, 138, 145, 146–7; and happiness, 35, 72, 82–3, 84, 159 n24; and judgment, 3, 13–14, 37; and moral examples, 2, 3–4; and moral value, 30–1; and priority of right over good, 69, 77, 78–80, 163 n9; and respect, 62; and universalizability, 9, 10, 26–7, 146–7; see also liberalism, Kantian
Kolnai, Aurel, 178 n14
Kuhn, Thomas, 156 n28

Lawrence, D. H., 21
Levi, Isaac, 179 n20
liberalism: Kantian, viii, xi, 47, 52, 72–3, 76, 77–85, 90, 91–2, 119, 120, 122, 124, 164 n20; as a modus vivendi, 73, 74–6, 90, 91, 121, 123–7; and neutrality, xi, 23, 42–7, 51–4, 66, 73–7, 90, 92, 98, 118, 129–30, see also neutrality; political doctrine, not a philosophy of man, viii, 25, 45, 46–7, 69, 70, 71, 74, 76, 92–3, 106, 118–19, 129
Locke, John, x, xi, 47, 76, 123, 130, 175 n77
Luhmann, Niklas, 107, 154 n2, 171 n34
Lukacs, Georg, 107, 170 n33

MacIntyre, Alasdair, x, 157 n6, 160 n32, 165 n25, 173 n51, 175 n71, 176 n1; diagnosis of modernity, 22, 24–7, 36–9, 157 n7; his "master argument", 28–33
Macpherson, C. B., 170 n30
Marx, Karl, 72, 76, 107–18, 170 n30, 171 n38, 172 n41–42, 173 n47
Mill, J. S., viii, 12, 51, 52, 106, 118, 129
modus vivendi, see liberalism, as a modus vivendi
Montesquieu, Charles Louis de Secondat de, 166 n1
morality: autonomous foundation of, 26, 28, 30–3, 137–8, 158 n18; see also ethics; obligations
Müller, Adam, 99

Nagel, Thomas, xi, 145–6, 166 n29, 176 n2, 179 n17
neo-Aristotelianism, see Arendt, Hannah; MacIntyre, Alasdair; Strauss, Leo
neutrality: justification of, 50–5, 59–61, 65–6, 122, 124, 161 n10–11; nature of, 43–7, 49–50, 69, 70, 74, 75, 118, 133, 144, 151, see also liberalism; practical limits to, 67–8
Novalis, 98–9
Nozick, Robert, 127

Oakeshott, Michael, 41
objectivity in ethics, xii, 27–30, 56, 58, 131, 149–50, 158 n14, 179 n17, 179 n22
obligations: categorical, ix, 79, 80, 84, 85, 86, 87, 89, 101; consequentialist, ix, 132, 134–9, 140–3, 144–50, 163 n9,

Index

CPSIA information can be obtained at www.ICGtesting.com
Printed in the USA
LVOW112139130612

286060LV00002B/38/A